D1610994

PANORAMAS OF PROMISE

Sherman and Mabel Smith Pettyjohn Lectures in Pacific Northwest History

PANORAMAS OF PROMISE

Pacific Northwest Cities and Towns on Nineteenth-Century Lithographs

John W. Reps

Washington State University Press
Pullman, Washington
1984

WSU
PRESS

Washington State University Press
Pullman, Washington

Library of Congress
Cataloging in Publication Data

Reps, John William
  Panoramas of Promise.
  Bibliography: p.
  1. Pacific, Northwest, in art. 2. Cities and Towns—Pacific, Northwest—
Views. 3. Lithography—19th century.
  I. Title

NE2454.R47 1984   769.499795   84-13164
ISBN 0-87422-016-5
ISBN 0-87422-017-3 (pbk.)

All illustrations are produced courtesy of the institutions and individuals indicated in the captions.

Panoramas of Promise was funded in part by grants from the Sherman and
Mabel Smith Pettyjohn Endowment at Washington State University; Lee J.
Sahlin, President, Murphy-Favre, Inc., Spokane; Stuart B. Bradley of Bradley,
McMurray, Black and Snyder, Chicago; and the Washington State University Foundation. Research upon which this work is based was underwritten
(in part) by a grant from the Program for Editions of the National Endowment for the Humanities, an independent federal agency.

FOREWORD

As the leading authority on the history of American urban planning, John W. Reps has made many contributions to specialized scholarship in that field. His publications include more than sixty book chapters, encyclopedia entries, and articles in conference proceedings and journals. Among the best known of his eight books are *The Making of Urban America: A History of City Planning in the United States* (1965), acclaimed for its innovative approach to urban history, and *Cities of the American West: A History of Frontier Urban Planning* (1979), which won the 1980 Albert J. Beveridge Prize of the American Historical Association as the best book in American history. The present volume is the result of several years of research that also produced the massive publication, *Views and Viewmakers of Urban America: Lithographs of Towns and Cities in the United States and Canada . . .* (1984), a comprehensive analysis and union catalog of 4,480 urban views listed by the specific states and provinces.

In *Panoramas of Promise* Reps brings his finely honed skills to bear on a single region once considered the "Far Corner" of the United States—the Pacific Northwest. Even in the 1840s, the early emigrants attracted to the Oregon country were town builders as well as farmers. Perhaps it was the promise of a great gateway for Oriental commerce, implicit in Manifest Destiny, that kept the urban vision alive, although the Asian trade failed to materialize immediately. Not until the 1880s when the transcontinental railroads ushered in a spectacular thirty-year boom period did the Pacific Northwest experience the impressive economic development and rapid population growth that would create an extensive townscape. At the beginning of the 1880s the sparsely settled region was overwhelmingly rural. Portland (population 17,500) was the only major city, while Walla Walla (3,588) was still slightly larger than Seattle (3,533). By 1910, however, Portland had jumped to 207,214, Seattle was a bustling metropolis of 234,194, and Spokane had skyrocketed from about 350 in 1880 to 104,402 thirty years later. In addition, the census of 1910 showed that Washington had become an urban state, with slightly more than half of its people living in towns and cities, and that Oregon was not far behind in urban growth.

Not surprisingly, the settlement of the Pacific Northwest during these boom decades required the founding of hundreds of new towns, some of which quickly became urban centers and thus exhibited the vitality as well as the foibles of the new region. Fortunately, a talented corps of itinerant artists roamed the Northwest, especially during the boom period 1880-1910, capturing the spirit of these raw, energetic communities in bird's-eye views that were widely circulated as lithographs. Through his prodigious research on this popular art form, which took him to archives and art museums from coast to coast, John Reps has given us a new perspective of the region's history and lifestyle. In addition to numerous illustrations and a detailed catalog of the artists and their Pacific Northwest works, the author provides pertinent information on the technology of lithography, as well as some practical lessons on the interpretation and evaluation of these urban views. Regardless of their artistic value, the historic lithographs are, as the author says, the best "single contemporary record" to portray "how Pacific Northwest frontier towns grew and changed and how they appeared to residents and visitors alike." And this remained so until well into the twentieth century when aerial photography superseded ground-level lithographic viewmaking as the best way to depict urban America.

John Reps's presentation on Pacific Northwest lithographs originated as a part of the Pettyjohn Lecture Series at Washington State University in the spring of 1983. The estate of Margaret Pettyjohn, a long-time Walla Walla area resident and patron of historical organizations, provided the University with an endowment designated for the promotion of Pacific Northwest history. The University of Washington and the University of Idaho also shared in the estate of Miss Pettyjohn, whose family farmed a large acreage near Prescott, Washington. She died in 1978. Beginning in the fall of 1980, the WSU Department of History started utilizing income from the Pettyjohn endowment to select visiting lecturers who have come to the Pullman campus for varying lengths of time. While at WSU, these nationally recognized specialists in some aspect of Pacific Northwest history have presented a major paper or a series of public lectures that are original contributions to knowledge and suitable for publication. The Pettyjohn Distinguished Lecturers have also conducted seminars and spoken in classes and colloquia. Some of the public lectures have been given in other cities of the state, thereby extending the benefits of the program beyond the WSU campus. In memory of Margaret Pettyjohn's parents, both pioneers of Walla

Walla County, the appointment is officially named the Sherman and Mabel Smith Pettyjohn Distinguished Lectureship of Pacific Northwest History. *Panoramas of Promise* is the first publication derived from the Pettyjohn Lecture Series.

Several other individuals and organizations have helped make this book possible. Lee J. Sahlin, President, Murphey-Favre, Inc., Spokane, and Stuart B. Bradley of Bradley, McMurray, Black & Snyder, Attorneys at Law, Chicago, gave their generous support. At Washington State University Albert C. Yates, Executive Vice President and Provost, Lois B. DeFleur, Dean, College of Sciences and Arts, and Connie H. Kravas, Executive Director of University Development and President of the WSU Foundation, provided encouragement as well as support; and at the WSU Press Thomas H. Sanders, Director of Publications and the WSU Press, Fredric C. Bohm, Managing Editor, and Christine Mercer, Designer, made even the most difficult problems work out smoothly. John R. Jameson, my colleague in the WSU History Department, had the acumen to nominate John Reps as a Pettyjohn Lecturer and then to outline the merits of this book. Finally, a grant from the National Endowment for the Humanities allowed Professor Reps to carry out a major portion of the research which contributed to this project.

David H. Stratton, Chairman
Department of History
Washington State University

TABLE OF CONTENTS

LIST OF ILLUSTRATIONS

From the beginning, Pacific Northwest settlement, like settlement elsewhere in Western America, involved the founding of scores of new towns. As these young communities became established urban centers, they served as markets for agricultural produce, wholesale and retail distribution outlets, political capitals, mining and supply points, sites for industries, railroad division depots, ocean and river ports, and locations for educational and other institutions. Urban places, as well as the rural expanses that surrounded them, thus played a vital role in the region's early development.[1]

Among the thousands of visitors attracted to the Pacific Northwest in the late nineteenth century were itinerant artists who recorded the appearance of these new communities. Ultimately their works were transformed into lithographs. Though many were published outside the region, first in California and the Midwest, they were later produced in Portland and a few other places in the region itself. In composition these urban views share some common traits. Most,

for example, show a town or city as if seen from high in the air, revealing street systems and patterns of open space, as well as depicting the features of individual buildings and neighborhoods. Better than any other single contemporary record, nineteenth-century lithographic urban views help us to visualize how Pacific Northwest frontier towns grew and changed and how they appeared to residents and visitors alike.[2]

The opportunities these prints offer for the study of urban places of the last century are not yet fully appreciated by scholars and students of the American West. This is unfortunate, for work done by these artists can provide information not available from other sources and supplement that which is obtained elsewhere—information needed by specialists in such disciplines as architectural history, historic preservation, urban geography, and the history of city planning and landscape architecture.

We can, for instance, look at a typical view, such as the lithograph showing Cheney, Washington, in 1884 (Figure 1). From it

we can reach conclusions about Cheney's size, shape, pattern, intensity of development, the way land was used, and how the town's buildings looked. It is obvious after seeing the illustration that Cheney was laid out on a comparatively level site in a gridiron pattern with streets running parallel to the railroad (in the foreground). These thoroughfares were intersected at right angles by lettered and named streets surveyed perpendicular to the tracks. The lithograph even identifies the railroad, the Northern Pacific line, and the numbered legend below the view lists the passenger and freight depots among Cheney's major structures (to the left of center). The business district of 1884 is easy to locate by its larger and more closely spaced buildings beyond the Oakes House, the large hotel facing the passenger station and whose proprietor the legend tells us was named McMurtough. Not far away, at the intersection of First and D streets, is the Commercial Hotel run by one John Norris.

False fronts concealing gabled roofs distinguish buildings used

Figure 1. *Cheney, Washington, 1884. (Geography and Map Division, Library of Congress) Catalog Number 78*

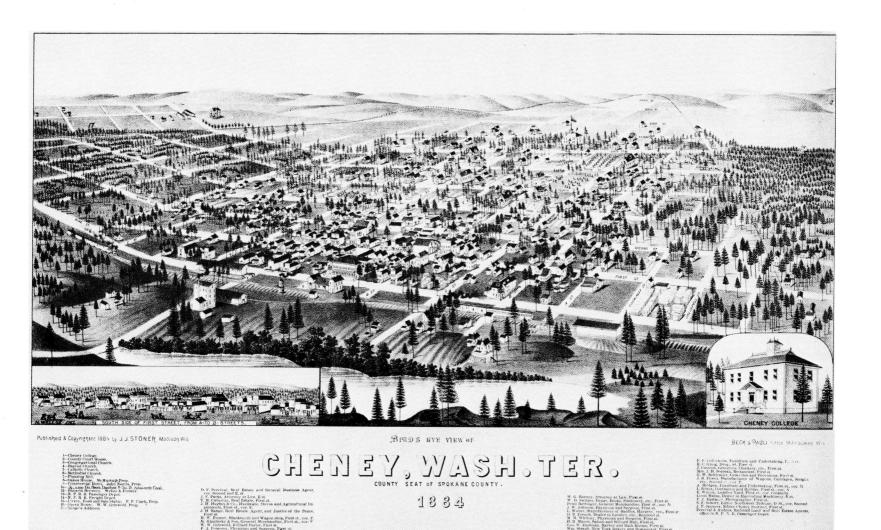

Figure 1. Cheney, Washington, 1884.

(Geography and Map Division, Library of Congress)

for business from those structures that were residences. Because the fronts of those buildings facing away from the contrived viewpoint cannot be seen, the artist included a long vignette (placed at the lower left corner of the print) showing these ''hidden'' elevations for six blocks of the business district concentrated along First Street. A magnifying glass is helpful in examining these prints. Close study reveals details of roof lines, windows, steps, porches, and other elements of architectural style which can be used in reaching conclusions about the age of buildings and the income and social status of their occupants.

Cheney could boast of four churches: Congregational, Baptist, Catholic, and Methodist. All stood on sites beyond Third Street in a portion of town that was only sparsely built up. This suggests that the churches may have been late arrivals on the urban scene or that the town's founder reserved sites for their use well away from the commercial heart of the city. Joining the houses of worship in this distant neighborhood were the county courthouse and—at the far edge of town facing Sixth Street— Benjamin P. Cheney Academy (identified in the legend as Cheney College), an institution that one would not expect to encounter so soon in what was a relatively new community founded in 1881.

We can deduce that in 1884 Cheney was a fairly new settlement by examining the pattern of trees. Nearly all of them are the same height and are less numerous at the center of town. Obviously those still standing are survivors of the pine forest that still thrives in the countryside surrounding this eastern Washington community. No new trees can be seen in the lithograph. What one can observe, however, are several blocks in the background near the courthouse and the Cheney Academy studded with tree stumps. This is a clue that the process of clearing the land for the town had begun not long before.

Cheney displayed an air of prosperity when this lithograph was done. The legend identifies a brewery and a flour mill, and their numbers allow us to find the locations near the railroad. W. W. Griswold's large opera house suggests that the residents had money to spend for entertainment. The four real estate agents listed in the legend, along with evidence from the view that the town's original blocks were augmented by a subdivision designated as Range's Addition, suggest that the place was growing.

The directory of local businesses is fairly long for a new town. These enterprises included a bank, a blacksmith and wagon shop, hardware, stove, and agricultural implement stores, a bakery, drug and grocery stores, restaurants, a photographer, a furniture store, a candy and tobacco shop, and two billiard parlors. Two lawyers and three physicians offered professional services, George Eastman ran a barbershop and bathhouse, and two newspapers informed Cheney residents of local and national events.

Figure 2 shows three diagrams locating some of the features of the town. Others could be noted, but these examples should be sufficient to demonstrate how helpful the views can be in revealing

Figure 2. *Major features of Cheney, Washington, in 1884. (John W. Reps)*

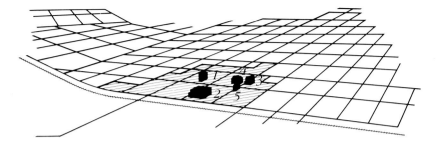

Major Features of Cheney, Washington in 1884.
(John W. Reps)

1. *Opera House*
2. *Oakes House*
3. *Commercial Hotel*
4. *Livery Stable*
5. *Bank*

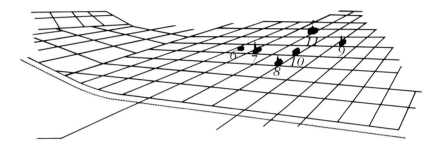

6. *Methodist Church*
7. *Congregational Church*
8. *Baptist Church*
9. *Catholic Church*
10. *Courthouse*
11. *Cheney College*

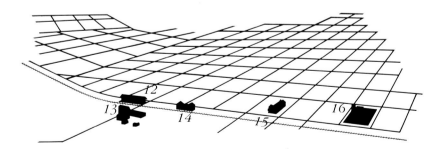

12. *Freight Depot*
13. *Flour Mill*
14. *Passenger Depot*
15. *Brewery*
16. *Lumber Yard*

Figure 2. Major Features of Cheney, Washington, in 1884.

(John W. Reps)

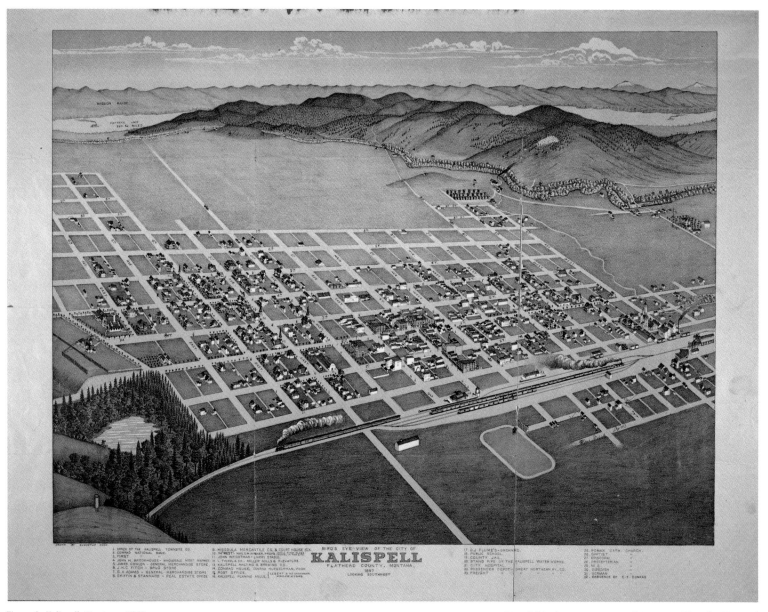

Figure 3. Kalispell, Montana, 1897.

THE AMERICAN VILLAGE

Figure 4. Oregon City, Oregon, 1846.

(Amon Carter Museum of Western Art, Fort Worth, Texas)

6

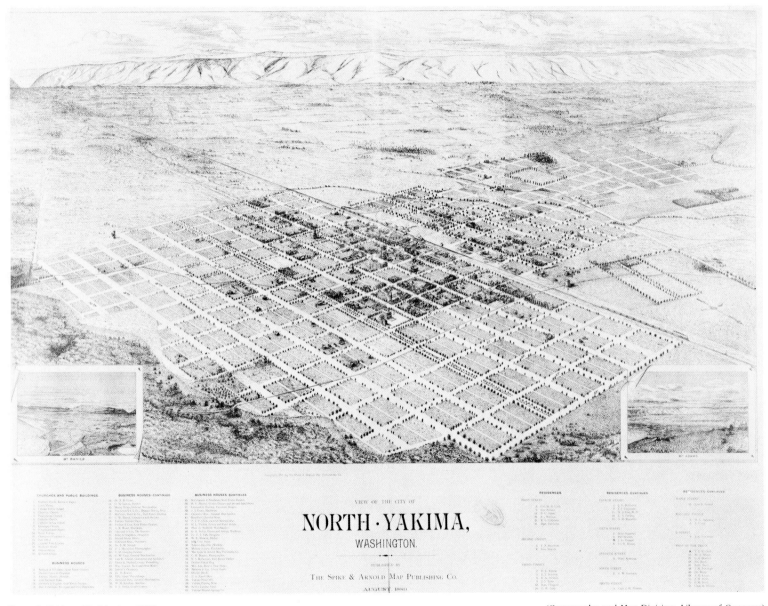

Figure 5. Yakima, Washington, 1889.

Figure 3. *Kalispell, Montana, 1897. (Mansfield Library, University of Montana, Missoula, Montana)* Catalog Number 25

Figure 4. *Oregon City, Oregon, 1846. (Amon Carter Museum of Western Art, Fort Worth, Texas)* Catalog Number 47

Figure 5. *Yakima, Washington, 1889. (Cartography and Map Division, Library of Congress)* Catalog Number 85

Figure 6. *Locations of towns and cities drawn by Kuchel & Dresel, Henry Wellge, and Eli S. Glover. (John W. Reps)*

Figure 7. *Portland, Oregon, 1890. (Bancroft Library, University of California, Berkeley, California)* Catalog Number 61

the basic physical structures of the places they depict.[3] This kind of analysis becomes even more valuable when used to compare two or more communities at the same period or in tracing changes taking place over time in a single community which was the subject of two or more views. More will be said about this point later.

One can approach these lithographs in other ways. For example, many private owners and print curators look on them fondly as antiquarian curiosities, perhaps even as perversely lovable illustrations of American nineteenth-century bad taste or of inadequate artistic abilities. Certainly examples of false and awkward perspective abound, such as the view of Kalispell, Montana (Figure 3). If projected into the distance, the town's street grid converges beyond the upper left and far right borders of the print. They are the vanishing points that the artist, Augustus Koch, used in preparing his drawing.

A conventional perspective has vanishing points on the horizon. Koch violated this rule by selecting his point at the left far above the horizon. The resulting distortion gives an observer the false impression that Kalispell is located on a steeply tilted plane. Koch, like other viewmakers, did this for commercial reasons; it allowed him to depict buildings in the background almost as large as similarly sized structures in the foreground. For an artist-publisher attempting to sell as many copies as possible, such a practice widened the market of potential customers who wished to see their place of business or residence clearly and accurately featured on the lithograph.[4]

Nineteenth-century urban views also provide evidence of changes in lithographic printing technology and in public attitudes toward art. The earliest lithograph of a town in the region shows Oregon City as drawn in 1846 by J. Henry Warre (Figure 4). In a manner to be explained presently, his sketch was put on lithographic stones in London and skillfully printed in several colors. This procedure gave the print the appealing character of a watercolor townscape. By contrast, Bruce Wellington Pierce's view of Portland in 1890—probably printed from zinc plates on a power press—combines an almost cartographic precision with the strong coloring of a modern poster (Figure 7). Pierce and his publishers clearly intended to capture attention by bold graphics rather than through artistic refinement and subtle suggestion.

One can also study the lithographs for their use in promoting urban land development, townsite speculation, and community pride. In 1885 the Northern Pacific Railroad platted 3,000 acres of land into streets and blocks to create what is now Yakima, Washington. The view (Figure 5) was published four years later and may have been commissioned by the railroad to lure new residents and to stimulate land sales. Even if not sponsored by the railroad, the lithograph most certainly was regarded favorably by Northern Pacific land agents as a device to call attention to their new community.[5]

When urban viewmakers came to town, local newspapers usually urged residents to support the publication of a proposed view. Nearly always they mentioned the promotional uses to which it might be put. For example, a Seattle journalist stated that Henry Wellge's lithograph of 1884 "will be a splendid thing to send abroad to advertise the town."[6] A Victoria, British Columbia, newspaper used the same approach in supporting the publication of Eli S. Glover's depiction of that community: "For reference, the view will prove invaluable to residents here, whilst for transmission to friends in England and elsewhere who have but a vague idea of the extent and beauty of our city, the picture will be found to be particularly adapted."[7]

Still another line of inquiry explores the paths of the itinerant artists and artist-publishers who produced most of these views and examines the graphic and business methods they employed in this uniquely American combination of art and commerce. Most of the lithographs of towns in the Pacific Northwest came from persons who learned the viewmaking business elsewhere. Usually these men visited the region only briefly as part of their efforts to produce and sell prints throughout the West or the entire country.[8] Figure 6 shows the locations of lithographs produced by Charles Kuchel, Emil Dresel, Eli S. Glover, and Henry Wellge. Although they were responsible for a substantial share of the region's views, most of their work took place in other parts of the continent.

These and other aspects of urban lithography can only be touched on in the pages that follow. We will examine first the long tradition of city viewmaking, indicate the impact of lithography on American artists, summarize the method of lithographic printing, and describe the techniques used by artists in drawing the cities they visited. We will then explore how all this came to be applied in the Pacific Northwest and conclude with examples of how the city perspectives can be utilized in tracing patterns of growth and change, selecting for this purpose several of the views of Seattle and Portland.

The tradition of printed city views began in Europe almost as early as printing itself. Hundreds of woodcuts embellished the pages of the *Nuremberg Chronicle*, published in 1493, most of them showing European towns and cities.[9] Sebastian Munster's *Cosmographae Universalis* of 1544 also included many detailed and less stylized woodcut illustrations of cities.[10] In 1572 Georg Braun and Franz Hogenberg issued the first volume of their atlas, *Civitates Orbis Terrarum*, consisting of hundreds of large and skillfully executed engravings of urban places in the Old World plus those of Cuzco and Mexico City in the New.[11]

In the seventeenth century Mathew Merian produced scores of finely detailed panoramas and high-level depictions of European cities, like that of Zurich in Figure 8. Dutch engravers, publishers, and mapmakers, such as Johannes Blaeu and Frederic de Wit, and the English historian and cartographer, John Speed, added to the many engraved city views available at that time.[12] While most appeared first as sheets bound in atlases or books of topographical description, others were sold separately to customers interested only in a single town or city.

Figure 8. *Zurich, Switzerland, in 1642. (John W. Reps)*

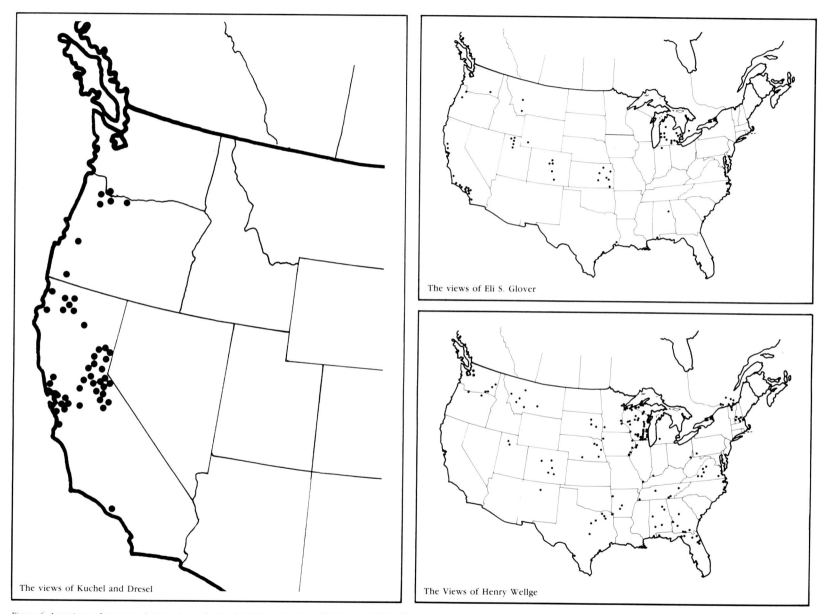

The views of Kuchel and Dresel

The views of Eli S. Glover

The Views of Henry Wellge

Figure 6. Locations of towns and cities drawn by Kuchel & Dresel, Henry Wellge, and Eli S. Glover.

(John W. Reps)

But this kind of illustration did not long remain confined to depicting European cities. From the beginning of American colonization, urban prints of towns in the New World proved popular in Europe. A few, such as Peter Gordon's engraving of Savannah in 1734, showed towns from points high in the air. More common were panoramas of cities as seen from ground or water level or from only a slightly elevated position, such as the print of New York as it appeared in 1736. Portions of both engravings are reproduced in Figure 9.

Artists in the United States generally used this panorama style for city views they produced as engravings or aquatints through the 1830s. William Guy Wall, John Hill, and William James Bennett—all from Britain—and George Cooke from Maryland were the most skilled and prolific of the early delineators of towns in the new republic. Their views, almost always found with the superb hand coloring of the period, are among the most sought-after of American historical prints because of their beauty and scarcity.[13]

Unfortunately, copperplate engraving and its aquatint variation required skills in short supply in nineteenth-century America. Lithography offered an easier method for creating images on paper. Invented in Bavaria by Alois Senefelder late in the eighteenth century, lithography had its first commercial use in the United States in the 1820s. The first views of towns printed in this country from lithographic stones were crude illustrations like that of Buffalo (in Figure 10) drawn by young George Catlin for a publication commemorating the opening of the Erie Canal in 1825.[14] So novel was the process that the editor of the volume felt obliged to provide his readers with a description of the art. A more detailed and accurate account of lithographic printing, however, appeared in 1826. It is worth quoting at length because, while oversimplified, it describes in easily understandable words how a lithograph was produced:

> The drawing is made on a polished stone, with an ink or chalk composed of greasy materials in the same way as drawings are executed on paper with common ink or chalk. The stone is then given to the lithographic printer, that he may obtain impressions from it. In order to do this, he wets the whole surface, but as the greasy materials, which constitute the drawing, will not receive water, only the uncovered part imbibes it. A thick greasy ink is then passed over the stone, and received by the lines of the drawing, while the remainder of the surface being wet refuses to take it. A sheet of paper is then pressed strongly on the stone, and a reversed impression of the drawing obtained. The stone is again wetted, again charged with ink, and thus a series of impressions are procured. The result is the same as in copperplate printing, but the means are different. The process of engraving is mechanical, that of lithography chemical.[15]

Figure 11 shows some of these and other steps involved in making a lithographic print. The person on the left is preparing the fine Bavarian limestones used in the process by rubbing stones together with a wet polishing compound between the two surfaces that will be used. Behind him, an artist is drawing on a prepared stone using greasy ink or chalk. The image had to be drawn in reverse, and artists sometimes used a mirror for this

Figure 9. *Savannah, Georgia, 1734 and New York City, 1736. Details. (Geography and Map Division, Library of Congress)*

Figure 10. *Buffalo, New York, 1825. (Olin Library, Cornell University, Ithaca, New York)*

Figure 11. *Interior of a lithographic printing shop. (American Antiquarian Society, Worcester, Massachusetts)*

Figure 7. Portland, Oregon, 1890.

purpose, although the artist in this illustration is not.

In the right foreground a stone with the drawing on it has been coated with a solution of diluted nitric or muriatic acid. This helps to keep the inked lines from spreading and makes the rest of the stone more receptive to water. After being sponged clean and thoroughly moistened, the stone is ready to be inked. The person with his back to us is doing this with a roller coated with printing ink, which is adhering only to the greasy lines drawn by the artist and is being repelled by the wet surface of stone elsewhere.

The printer will then put a sheet of paper on the stone, cover it with a protective leather mat, and adjust the scraper bar above the center of the press. Using a crank, he will move the stone under the bar to exert heavy pressure and thus transfer the printing ink from the stone to the paper. He will then carefully remove the paper and hang it to dry while inking the stone once again to repeat the process. In the background we can see a printer feeding sheets of paper to a power press which eventually replaced the early hand presses.[16]

Lithographs printed in color required the use of additional stones, one for each color. A simple elaboration often used by publishers of urban views involved a second stone inked with orange-brown or grey-green ink. This tone stone provided sky and shadow details and was also commonly used for borders and to decorate the title. Each such lithograph thus passed through the press twice, once on a stone inked in black ink and again when a tone stone impression was added.

Eli Glover's rendering of Oregon's capital city of Salem in 1876 is a good example of this technique. Even in the black and white illustration (Figure 12), one can see how Glover (or some anonymous lithographer at his San Francisco printer) used the tone stone to create a dramatic sky, as well as to enrich the appearance of the woods in the foreground and around the outskirts of the city.

Three or more stones made it possible to create a print having the appearance of being fully colored. Lithographers achieved this effect by printing one color over another to derive a third. They used a stone inked with blue ink to produce sky and water and also those parts of the print that were to appear green. They used a stone inked with orange-brown ink for streets and shadowed facades of buildings, but it, too, was employed on portions of the view that were meant to be green. Overprinting of blue with orange-brown produced the desired green for lawns, shrubs, and trees.[17]

Bruce Wellington Pierce's illustration of Portland in 1890 (Figure 7) shows the effects of what could be achieved with multiple colors. The printer, W. W. Elliott, seems to have used separate colors rather than deriving them through overprinting. By 1890, when Pierce drew the view, zinc plates had replaced stones at many presses; it is also possible that Elliott used photographic methods, at least in part, when he prepared the various plates. The only problem remaining was to obtain good registration each time the paper passed

Figure 12. *Salem, Oregon, 1876. (Geography and Map Division, Library of Congress) Catalog Number 70*

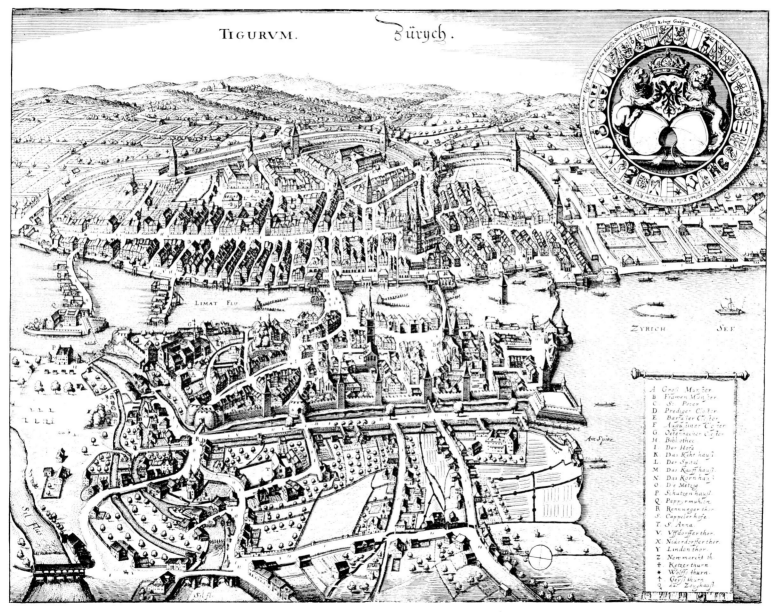

Figure 8. Zurich, Switzerland in 1642.

(John W. Reps)

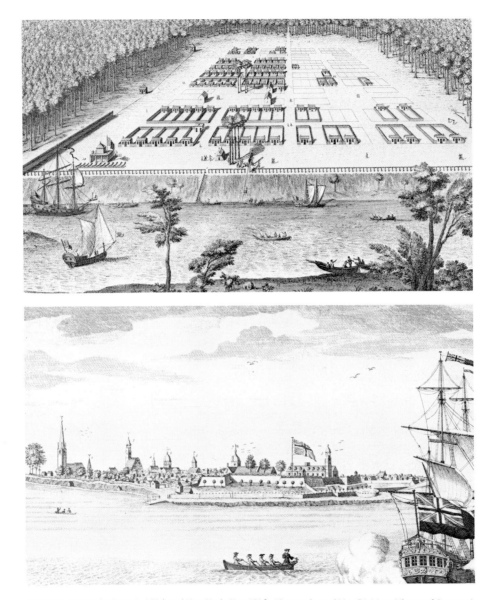

Figure 9. Savannah, Georgia, 1734, and New York City, 1736. (Geography and Map Division, Library of Congress)

BUFFALO FROM THE LIGHT HOUSE.

Figure 10. Buffalo, New York, 1825.

(Olin Library, Cornell University, Ithaca, New York)

LITHOGRAPHER.

Figure 11. Interior of a lithographic printing shop.

(American Antiquarian Society, Worcester, Massachusetts)

Figure 12. Salem, Oregon, 1876.

through the press so that the colors would be exactly positioned with neither overlaps nor gaps.[18]

Very few lithographs of cities in the Pacific Northwest were hand colored at this time. Those now found with such embellishment in private or institutional collections were almost surely colored in our own era. The impression of Eli Glover's view of Olympia (Figure 14) is an excellent example of skillful, although modern, coloring. Other impressions of this lithograph are known in the form in which it was sold at the time: as a toned print with grey-green ink creating cloud and shadow effects and being used as well for the border and in the title.[19]

It may be easier to understand how lithographs were printed than to imagine the process by which artists created their original images. Although on Glover's view of Salem (Figure 12) one finds the statement that it was "drawn by E. S. Glover from S. A. Smith's photograph," it is obvious to anyone who has visited the city that there is no place Smith could have placed his camera to observe a scene like the one Glover drew. Nor is there any record of balloons in the sky of Salem or any other city of the region at the time these drawings were made.[20] The artist's perspective, therefore, was entirely imaginary. This is true for all of the views of cities portrayed from high overhead, including those—like Glover's lithographs of Olympia (Figure 14) and Port Townsend, Washington (Figure 13)—that show hills in the foreground to give the impression that it was here the artist stood to sketch the scene below. Instead, the completion of such a view required more painstaking work than merely setting up an easel and recording the appearance of the town from a distance.

Glover, like his fellow viewmakers of the time, began by moving slowly through the town and making dozens of ground-level sketches of individual buildings and landscape features. He doubtless used whatever photographic or printed images that already existed. If he had limited time, he may have commissioned additional photographs of major buildings that he could use to draw from at his leisure or when the weather did not permit outdoor sketching. The artist also certainly would have examined any earlier views available to him.[21]

Glover then used a street map to construct a perspective grid, fixing his imaginary viewpoint and vanishing points so the town would appear as if seen from the orientation and elevation he had determined. From field sketches he then redrew the structures on the perspective, taking care to make each building the correct size and to locate it properly within the block where it could be found.

Figure 15 is a detail from such a drawing. It was the work of Bruce Wellington Pierce in 1894 when he drew Los Angeles. Pierce must have produced similar intermediate drawings for his lithographs of Portland and Walla Walla, among the cities he portrayed in the Pacific Northwest. After making corrections and adding new material to this preliminary work, the artist then prepared a more attractive and carefully rendered final drawing. He used this version for display

Figure 13. *Port Townsend, Washington, 1878. (Geography and Map Division, Library of Congress)*
Catalog Number 91

Figure 14. *Olympia, Washington, 1879. (Amon Carter Museum of Western Art, Fort Worth, Texas)*
Catalog Number 86

Figure 15. *Sketches of a portion of Los Angeles, California, by Bruce Wellington Pierce, circa 1894. (Special Collections, University of Washington Libraries, Seattle, Washington)*

Drawn and Published by E. S. Glover, Portland, Oregon.

Entered according to Act of Congress, in the year 1878, by E. S. Glover, in the Office of the Librarian of Congress, at Washington, D. C.

A. L. Bancroft & Co., Lith., San Francisco, Cal.

BIRD'S EYE VIEW OF
PORT TOWNSEND,
PUGET SOUND, WASHINGTON TERRITORY.

FROM THE NORTH-EAST.

1878.

A.—Presbyterian Church.
B.—Methodist Church.
C.—Episcopal Church.
D.—Catholic Church.
E.—Cosmopolitan Hotel.

F.—Masonic Building.
G.—Odd Fellows' Hall.
H.—Good Templars' Hall.
I.—Red Men's Hall.
J.—Public School.

K.—Post Office.
L.—Court House.
M.—Jail Building.
N.—Custom House.
O.—Dr. Hill's Drug Store.

P.—Democratic Press.
Q.—Weekly Argus.
R.—Rothschild & Co., Shipping Merchants.
S.—Fort Townsend.
T.—Olimp Mountains.

Figure 13. Port Townsend, Washington, 1878.

(Amon Carter Museum of Western Art, Fort Worth, Texas)

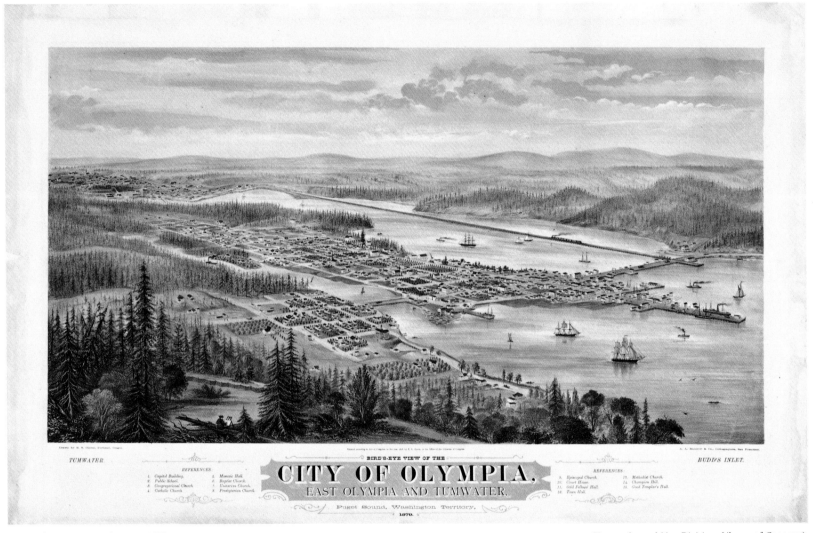

TUMWATER

REFERENCES

1. Capitol Building.   5. Masonic Hall.
2. Public School.   6. Baptist Church.
3. Congregational Church. 7. Unitarian Church.
4. Catholic Church.   8. Presbyterian Church.

=BIRD'S-EYE VIEW OF THE=

CITY OF OLYMPIA,

EAST OLYMPIA AND TUMWATER,

Puget Sound, Washington Territory,

1879.

REFERENCES

9. Episcopal Church.   12. Methodist Church.
10. Court House.   13. Champion Hall.
11. Odd Fellows Hall.   14. Good Templar's Hall.
15. Town Hall.

BUDD'S INLET.

Figure 14. Olympia, Washington, 1879.

(Geography and Map Division, Library of Congress)

21

Figure 15. Sketches of a portion of Los Angeles, California, by Bruce Wellington Pierce, circa 1894. (Special Collections, University of Washington Libraries, Seattle, Washington)

purposes when soliciting subscriptions from townspeople for the eventual lithograph. The artist also sent or took this rendition to the lithographer to be copied on stone if the artist did not do so himself. An example of one such drawing from the Pacific Northwest is reproduced in Figure 16. This depiction was the basis for a view of Portland published in 1904, a lithograph to be illustrated and described presently.

The preparation of field sketches as the artist's beginning stage explains why even small details of individual buildings appear so accurately portrayed on their tiny images in the lithographs. Figure 17 provides an example. It shows sketches made by Edwin Whitefield for his view of Quincy, Massachusetts, in 1877 and a portion of the lithograph containing the same images. Note the close similarity to the way Whitefield depicted the estates of John Quincy Adams and Charles Francis Adams in his sketches and how they appear in much smaller size on the print. All the essential architectural features are identical.

Although this was the technique used for most views produced after the Civil War, the pioneer artists of the Pacific Northwest employed instead the more conventional approach of academic townscape painting. In such pictures the towns appear as if sitting for a portrait at the level of the artist's eye or as seen from a slight elevation. Captain Henry J. Warre's impression of Oregon City (Figure 4) is one example of this approach.

The earliest separately issued lithographs of the region to be printed in America also imitated this style of easel painting. They were produced in San Francisco from drawings made by or for the firm of Kuchel & Dresel. Figure 18 depicts their initial view of a town in the Pacific Northwest: the mining community of Jacksonville, Oregon, as it appeared in 1856. The viewmakers, Charles Kuchel and Emil Dresel, both Europeans, came to California during the Gold Rush. They found no gold but remained to record the appearance of most of the towns in the mining region extending through California to southern Oregon.

In 1858 and 1859 Kuchel & Dresel produced views of Vancouver, Washington (Figure 19), and five places in Oregon, including Oregon City (Figure 20).[22] These lithographs of towns in their early years of existence are typical of the Kuchel & Dresel style. They provide a representation of the entire place as seen from a distance and from only a slight elevation. Vignettes surrounding the principal scene provide details of the community's major buildings.[23]

For architectural historians, specialists in preservation, or persons seeking to trace successive uses of significant features, these border vignettes offer fascinating and instructive glimpses of early building styles and business activities. A sampling of the vignettes found on the Kuchel & Dresel lithograph of Portland provides a good example (Figure 21). These introduce us to a saloon, livery stables, a bakery, furniture store, church, school, jail, firehouse, and hotel. A bookstore and a stove shop, with an Odd Fellows Hall overhead, are among several other office buildings and retail stores of unspecified use.

Figure 16. *Manuscript drawing for a view of Portland, Oregon, in 1904. (Oregon Historical Society, Portland, Oregon)*

Figure 17. *Sketches by Edward Whitefield for a view of Quincy, Massachusetts, in 1870 with corresponding portions of lithograph. (Private collection)*

Figure 18. *Jacksonville, Oregon, circa 1856. (Amon Carter Museum of Western Art, Fort Worth, Texas)*
Catalog Number 43

Figure 19. *Vancouver, Washington, 1858. (Amon Carter Museum of Western Art, Fort Worth, Texas)*
Catalog Number 121

Figure 20. *Oregon City, Oregon, 1858. (Amon Carter Museum of Western Art, Fort Worth, Texas)*
Catalog Number 49

Figure 16. Manuscript drawing for a view of Portland, Oregon, in 1904.

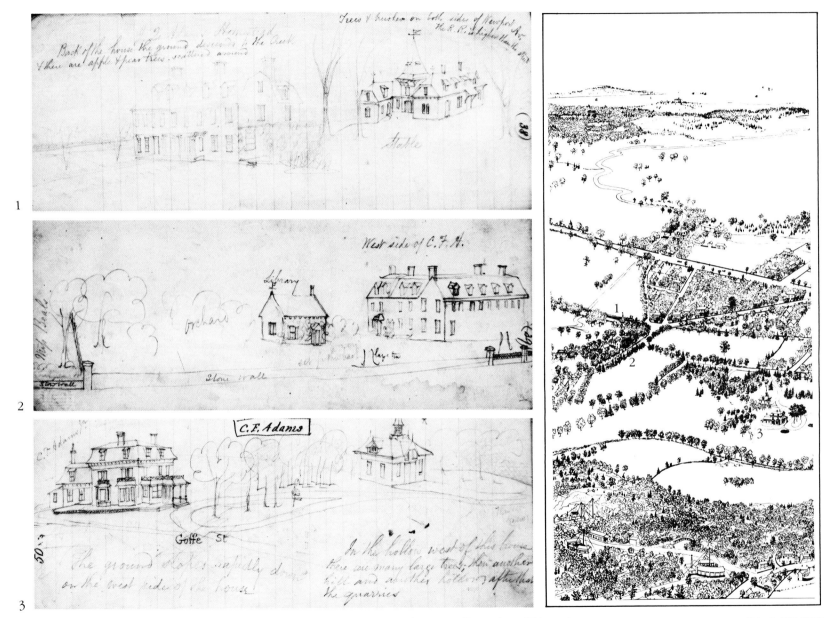

Figure 17. Sketches by Edward Whitefield for a view of Quincy, Massachusetts, in 1870 with corresponding portions of lithograph.

(Private collection)

25

Figure 18. Jacksonville, Oregon, circa 1856.

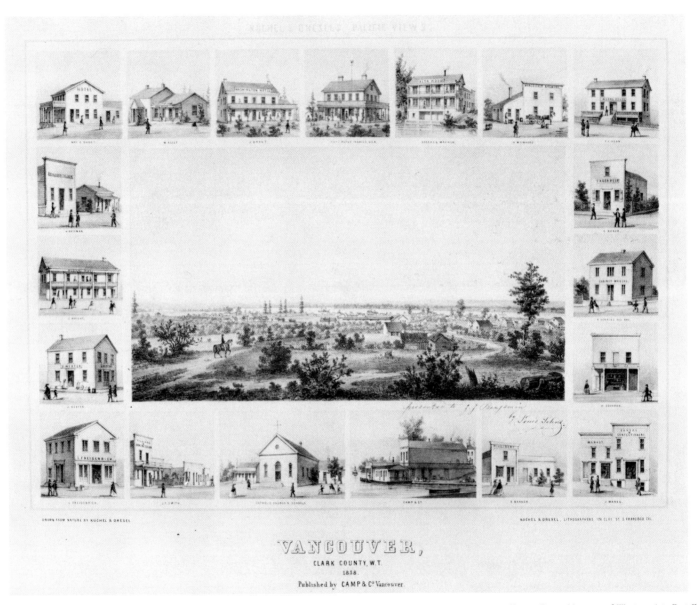

Figure 19. Vancouver, Washington, 1858.

Figure 20. Oregon City, Oregon, 1858.

(Amon Carter Museum of Western Art, Fort Worth, Texas)

Others followed Kuchel & Dresel in exploiting the market for urban views in the Pacific Northwest. Grafton Tyler Brown, a black artist, painter, and publisher from San Francisco, produced an early Portland drawing that imitated the style and vignette format made popular by his California predecessors. His work (Figure 22) was put on stone by Charles Kuchel, and was published about 1861.

Brown printed and probably drew three other city views of the region. Two appeared in 1866. One shows Silver City, Idaho, and the other Walla Walla (Figure 23). An Astoria, Oregon, lithograph followed about 1870.[24] All three include in their imprints a statement that they were made from photographs by P. F. Castleman. A notice in the Walla Walla *Statesman* for May 5, 1865, gives further confirmation: "Mr. P. F. Castleman is engaged in taking photographic views of the city and of the principal business houses, with a view of sending them to San Francisco and having them lithographed."[25]

Brown probably found the photographs of greatest use in preparing the vignettes—thirty of them in the case of the Walla Walla print. The newspaper account of the pending publication of this view is particularly revealing about one aspect of these smaller and more detailed illustrations. Its author informed his readers that "those who have their places of business or residences" depicted "in the margin" were expected to pay "a stipulated sum for the same." We know, therefore, that in addition to income derived from selling the lithographs themselves, their publishers received fees from those who wished their houses, stores, or factories to be singled out for special attention.[26]

Following the Civil War the artists engaged in urban portraiture shifted their imaginary viewpoints to show their subjects as if seen from high in the air. Illustrations of this type combine cartographic and pictorial qualities. Although we cannot scale distances from them directly, they reveal street patterns, relative sizes of lots, relationships between major land uses, the location of public buildings and open spaces, and many other elements of the physical structure of urban communities.

In this period many more itinerant artists and artist-publishers came to the Pacific Northwest to meet the increased demand for city views. Most of these visitors had learned their craft in the Midwest. One of them was Eli S. Glover, who began as a sales agent and assistant for another artist before striking out on his own, first as a printer in Chicago and then—following the destruction of his business by fire—as an independent viewmaker.

Glover spent some time in Nebraska, moved west to Colorado, and then stopped for awhile in Utah to draw its towns and cities. After sketching for a view of Helena, Montana, he set out on horseback for Walla Walla where he arrived in the fall of 1875. He stopped long enough to record its buildings for a lithograph published the following year (Figure 24). Glover paused briefly in Salem, Oregon (Figure 12), before continuing his voyage to California by sea. His handsome prints of these places came from the San Francisco press of

Figure 21. Portland, Oregon, 1858. Detail. (Amon Carter Museum of Western Art, Fort Worth, Texas) Catalog Number 53

Figure 22. Portland, Oregon, circa 1861. (Amon Carter Museum of Western Art, Fort Worth, Texas) Catalog Number 54

Figure 23. Walla Walla, Washington, 1866. (Northwest Archives, Whitman College, Walla Walla, Washington) Catalog Number 124

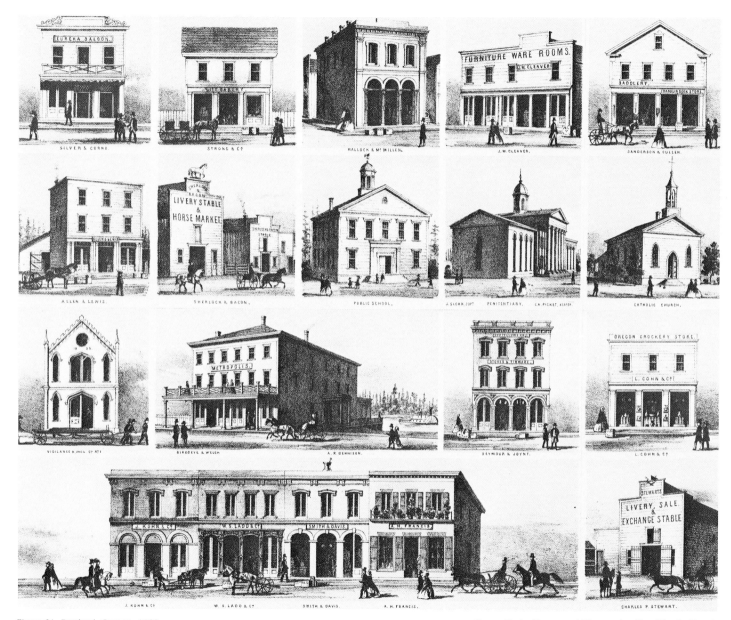

Figure 21. Portland, Oregon, 1858.

Figure 22. Portland, Oregon, circa 1861.

Figure 23. Walla Walla, Washington, 1866.

A. L. Bancroft & Co., an experienced and skilled firm that printed many other views that Glover drew.

Late in 1877 Glover moved to Portland where he lived for two years while preparing drawings of towns in the region. These works included detailed and attractive lithographs of Seattle in 1878 and Portland in 1879, both of which will be discussed later, as well as his fine vista of Washington's capital, Olympia (Figure 14). In that print Glover incorporated a bit of foreground detail to lend an air of realism to the scene and improve its composition. He used the figure of an artist working at his easel, presumably a self-portrait.[27]

Among Glover's works is a print of Tacoma in 1878, the place founded five years earlier as the future deep-water terminus of the Northern Pacific Railroad. Reproduced in Figure 25, the lithograph shows the town still at the beginning of its growth which had been throttled by the panic of 1873. Glover managed to give it a busy air, nonetheless, using locomotive and factory smoke to suggest a level of business and industrial activity that the little community of perhaps six hundred persons probably did not enjoy until a few years later.

Glover's evident success in selling his works may have encouraged others to visit the region. In 1880 Henry Steinegger, head of the San Francisco firm that printed Glover's work, toured the mining area of Idaho and drew the communities of Rocky Bar (Figure 26) and Quartzburgh. Steinegger's prints provide rare glimpses of mining camp life in Idaho, an area passed over by most itinerant viewmakers.

Four years later, in 1884, the energetic Henry Wellge traveled through the Pacific Northwest to sketch places such as Missoula, Montana (Figure 27), and Cheney, Washington (Figure 1), the latter of which we have analyzed previously. Joseph J. Stoner of Madison, Wisconsin, published Wellge's views, having them printed in Milwaukee by Beck & Pauli, a firm specializing in this craft. Stoner had been associated as business agent and publisher with several other view artists who began their careers in and around Wisconsin where Wellge evidently settled after coming to America from Germany.

One of his sales agents later claimed that Wellge once served as "captain in the engineering corps of the Russian Army."[28] While this may not have been true, there is an engineering-like precision in his drafting, as well as in the meticulous listing of churches, industries, hotels, business enterprises, and professional offices that one finds in the long and informative legends appearing on most of his prints. Those of Dayton, Washington (Figure 28), and Pendleton, Oregon (Figure 29), provide additional examples of his style.[29]

In addition to his eastern Washington lithographs of Cheney, Dayton, and Walla Walla, Wellge also included one of Spokane. His likeness of the future "Hub of the Inland Empire" (Figure 30) captures the city as seen from above the Spokane River and looks down the tumbling falls that supplied energy for the first industries. In the background Wellge drew the railroad that linked this once-isolated

Figure 24. *Walla Walla, Washington, 1876. (Geography and Map Division, Library of Congress) Catalog Number 125*

Figure 25. *Tacoma, Washington, 1878. (Geography and Map Division, Library of Congress) Catalog Number 112*

Figure 26. *Rocky Bar, Idaho, circa 1880. (Idaho State Historical Society, Boise, Idaho) Catalog Number 20*

Figure 27. *Missoula, Montana, 1884. (Amon Carter Museum of Western Art, Fort Worth, Texas) Catalog Number 26*

Figure 28. *Dayton, Washington, 1884. (Geography and Map Division, Library of Congress) Catalog Number 79*

Figure 29. *Pendleton, Oregon, 1884. (Amon Carter Museum of Western Art, Fort Worth, Texas) Catalog Number 50*

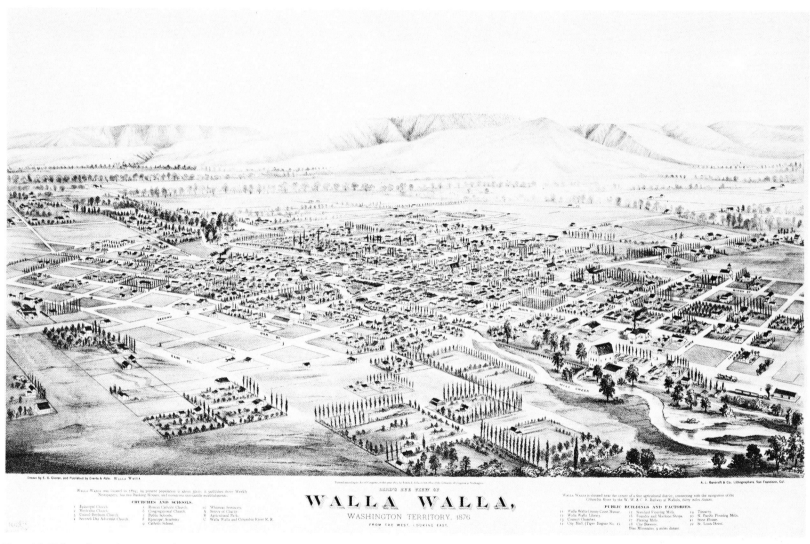

Drawn by E. S. Glover, and Published by Everts & Able, WALLA WALLA

Entered according to Act of Congress, in the year 1876, by Everts & Able, in the office of the Librarian of Congress at Washington

A. L. Bancroft & Co., Lithographers, San Francisco, Cal.

WALLA WALLA was located in 1859, its present population is about 4000; it publishes three Weekly Newspapers, has two Banking Houses, and numerous mercantile establishments.

BIRD'S EYE VIEW OF

WALLA WALLA,

WASHINGTON TERRITORY, 1876.

FROM THE WEST, LOOKING EAST.

WALLA WALLA is situated near the centre of a fine agricultural district, connecting with the navigation of the Columbia River by the W. W. & C. R. Railway at Wallula, thirty miles distant.

CHURCHES AND SCHOOLS.

1 Episcopal Church.
2 Methodist Church.
3 United Brethren Church.
4 Seventh Day Adventist Church.

5 Roman Catholic Church.
6 Congregational Church.
7 Public Schools.
8 Episcopal Academy.
9 Catholic School.

10 Whitman Seminary.
A Sisters of Charity.
B Agricultural Park.
C Walla Walla and Columbia River R. R.

PUBLIC BUILDINGS AND FACTORIES.

11 Walla Walla County Court House.
12 Walla Walla Library.
13 Council Chamber.
14 City Hall, (Tiger Engine No. 2).

15 Standard Flouring Mills.
16 Foundry and Machine Shops.
17 Planing Mills.
18 City Brewery.
Blue Mountains, 9 miles distant.

19 Tannery.
20 N. Pacific Flouring Mills.
21 Stine House.
22 St. Louis Hotel.

Figure 24. Walla Walla, Washington, 1876.

(Geography and Map Division, Library of Congress)

34

VIEW OF

NEW TACOMA AND MOUNT RAINIER,

Puget Sound, Washington Territory.

TERMINUS OF THE NORTHERN PACIFIC RAILROAD.

Altitude of Mount Rainier 14,440 feet.

Figure 25. Tacoma, Washington, 1878.

Figure 26. Rocky Bar, Idaho, circa 1880.   (Idaho State Historical Society, Boise, Idaho)

BIRD'S EYE VIEW OF

MISSOULA MON.

COUNTY SEAT OF MISSOULA COUNTY.

1884

RAIL ROAD SHOPS TO BE BUILT THIS SUMMER

SOUTH SIDE OF FRONT STREET.

SOUTH SIDE OF FRONT STREET.

Figure 27. Missoula, Montana, 1884.

(Amon Carter Museum of Western Art, Fort Worth, Texas)

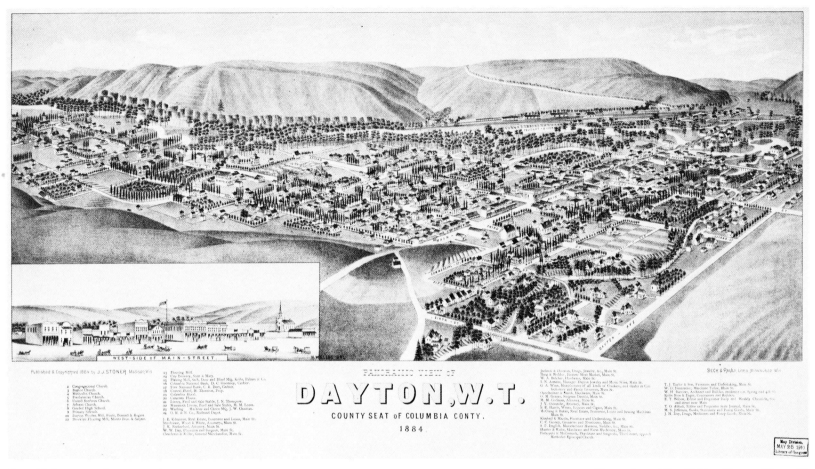

Figure 28. Dayton, Washington, 1884.

(Geography and Map Division, Library of Congress)

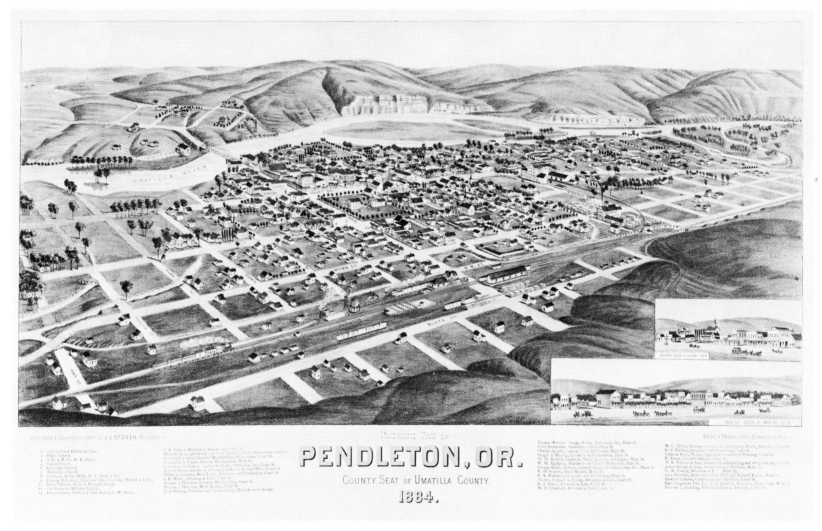

PENDLETON, OR.

COUNTY SEAT OF UMATILLA COUNTY.

1884.

Figure 29. Pendleton, Oregon, 1884.

(Amon Carter Museum of Western Art, Fort Worth, Texas)

Figure 30. Spokane, Washington, 1884.

location with the East and transformed the town of 350 people in 1880 to a boom community growing wealthy as the supply center for the Coeur d'Alene mining region just beyond the nearby Idaho border.

Henry Wellge must have been a busy man a century ago, for in addition to his drawings of Missoula, Cheney, Walla Walla, Dayton, Pendleton, and Spokane, he also produced views of Seattle and Tacoma in 1884 (Figure 31). By comparing Wellge's Tacoma lithograph with Glover's work of just six years earlier (Figure 25), one can see that the town's growth had been particularly swift; its experience demonstrated the importance of rail transportation in the race for urban supremacy. When Wellge drew the city, the Northern Pacific still had another three years before completing its transcontinental line, but Tacoma prospered from the promise of the future and a connection eastward via other railroads. To receive expected visitors the Tacoma Hotel had opened its doors in 1884. From this building, designed by the distinguished

eastern architectural firm of McKim, Mead, and White, guests could look out from its commanding site on a bluff above the water to a busy harbor below.

Two artists from California who began to draw cities during the land boom of the 1880s in and around Los Angeles also ventured northward at the end of the decade seeking new subjects for their lithographs. The first was E. S. Moore in 1890, who sketched three Oregon towns: Ashland (Figure 32), Grants Pass, and Salem. Since these were the only views outside of California that Moore produced, it seems likely that he found this venture unprofitable.

Moore's contemporary, Bruce Wellington Pierce, was more prolific and was also responsible for more interesting and important lithographs. Perhaps Pierce arrived by ship from Los Angeles and stopped in Astoria just long enough in 1889 to draw the view reproduced in Figure 34. Among the vignettes surrounding his high-level depiction of the town are several showing interiors of business and industrial establishments. In the legend, sixty numbered references furnish a guide to the locations of virtually all aspects of life in Astoria.

Pierce moved up the Columbia River and overland to Walla Walla to add his version of that city (Figure 33) to those already provided by Grafton Brown, Eli Glover, and Henry Wellge. It is thus possible for one to trace the growth and change of this community using four views spanning a little more than two decades. In this respect Walla Walla, although of modest size, rivals the larger late nineteenth-century centers of Portland, Seattle, and Tacoma.

It must have taken Pierce many weeks of work in 1890 to complete his most ambitious project to date, the large and almost excessively detailed depiction of Portland, then the region's most populous and intensely developed metropolis. The long legend of this view (Figure 7), its many vignettes, and the several scenes of building interiors are all typical of Pierce's attempts to make his views more attractive to potential customers and thus profitable to himself and his publishers.

Figure 30. *Spokane, Washington, 1884. (Manuscripts, Archives and Special Collections, Washington State University Libraries, Pullman, Washington) Catalog Number 106*

Figure 31. *Tacoma, Washington, 1884. (Geography and Map Division, Library of Congress) Catalog Number 113*

Figure 32. *Ashland, Oregon, 1890. (Southern Oregon Historical Society, Jacksonville, Oregon) Catalog Number 30*

Figure 33. *Walla Walla, Washington, 1890. (Northwest Archives, Whitman College, Walla Walla, Washington) Catalog Number 128*

Figure 31. Tacoma, Washington, 1884.

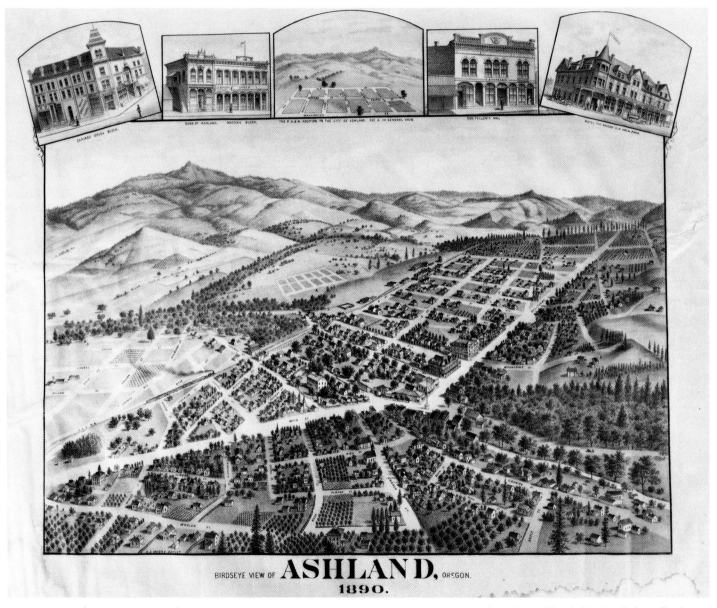

BIRDSEYE VIEW OF **ASHLAND,** OREGON.
1890.

Figure 32. Ashland, Oregon, 1890.

(Southern Oregon Historical Society, Jacksonville, Oregon)

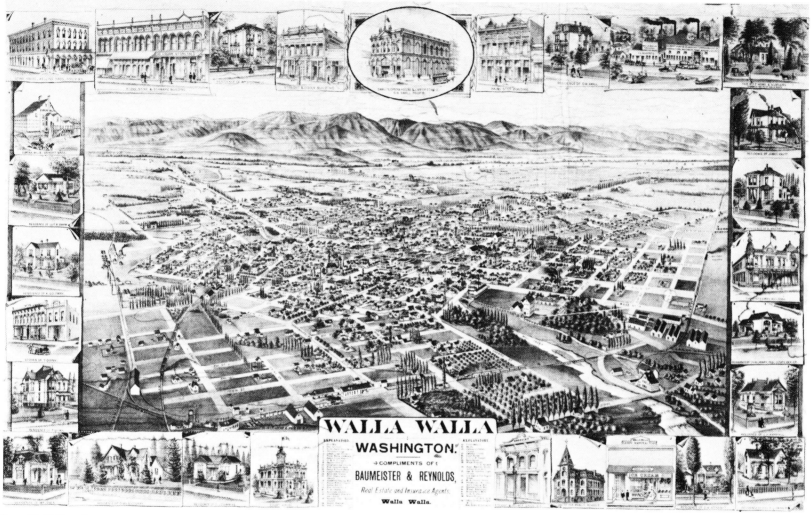

Figure 33. Walla Walla, Washington, 1890.

(Northwest Archives, Whitman College, Walla Walla, Washington)

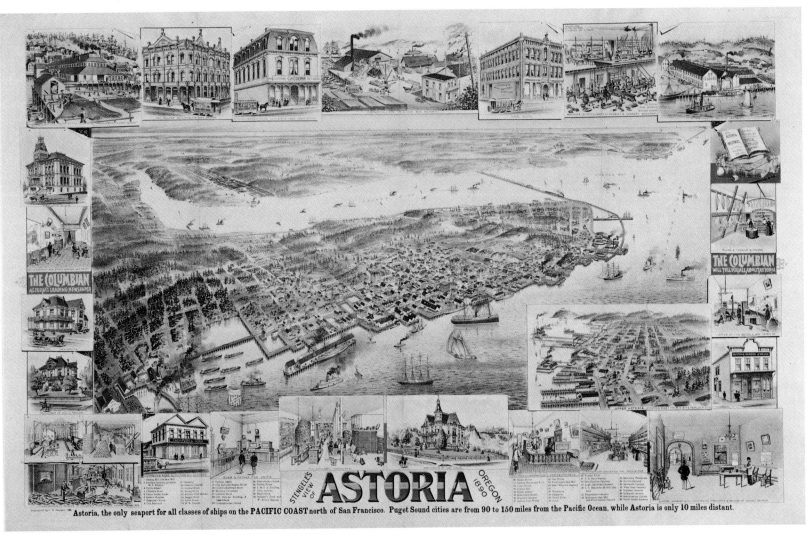

Figure 34. Astoria, Oregon, 1890.

(Amon Carter Museum of Western Art, Fort Worth, Texas)

Figure 34. *Astoria, Oregon, 1890. (Amon Carter Museum of Western Art, Fort Worth, Texas) Catalog Number 35*

Figure 35. *Fairhaven, Washington (now part of Bellingham, Washington), 1891. (State Historical Society of Wisconsin, Madison, Wisconsin) Catalog Number 82*

Figure 36. *Moscow, Idaho, 1897. (University of Idaho Library, Moscow, Idaho) Catalog Number 18*

Figure 37. *Spokane, Washington [1888]. (Oregon Historical Society, Portland, Oregon) Catalog Number 108*

During his tour of the region, Pierce visited Bellingham Bay in 1891 to sketch the new town founded only eight years earlier as Fairhaven, now a part of the City of Bellingham, Washington. Probably the Fairhaven Land Company, whose name appears on the imprint, sponsored Pierce's work to help promote its real estate venture. Note that this print (Figure 35) has no legend, possibly an indication that it shows imaginary or proposed buildings. This was true of many of the land boom lithographs of southern California where Pierce had established his reputation.[30]

One other national artist of urban lithographs came to the Pacific Northwest before the demand for prints of this type dwindled under the impact of photography, the reproduction of images by the halftone process, the rise of illustrated magazines and newspapers, and changes in popular taste. This was Augustus Koch, who, like Glover and Wellge, roamed the country drawing cities. His view-making career began in 1868 and continued for thirty years. In 1897, the year before he did his last lithograph, he produced views of Kalispell, Montana (Figure 3), and Moscow, Idaho (Figure 36).

Doubtless Koch worked with great speed, sketching individual buildings, consulting photographs and printed images, constructing a suitable perspective grid, and completing his final drawing for local display as a means to obtain advance subscriptions for the finished lithograph. Long practice would have made these tasks almost automatic, for by this time Koch had produced well over one hundred similar views of places in twenty-three states extending from Virginia to California and from Maine to Florida. Koch used few vignettes on his views, and for his Moscow print he selected for this purpose only the building where five years earlier the first forty students admitted to the new state university began their classes.

Koch, Wellge, and Glover—all with Midwestern origins as viewmakers—and Californians, such as Charles Kuchel and Emil Dresel, E. S. Moore, and Bruce Wellington Pierce, produced the bulk of the views of cities in the Pacific Northwest. Most of the other prints, like J. T. Pickett's lithograph of Spokane in 1888 (Figure 37), came either from local artists or from visitors with no previous or subsequent record as view artists.

The single most important source of city views within the region was the *West Shore*, a magazine based in Portland. It began in 1875 and continued for fifteen years. Its owner and editor, Leopold Samuel, dedicated himself to trumpeting the beauties, virtues, and commercial advantages of the northwest corner of the nation in general and Oregon in particular. Samuel embellished the magazine's pages with many lithographic views, some printed with a single additional tone and others with two or more tones. Most of these illustrations featured individual buildings or street scenes of towns and cities described in the accompanying text. Several illustrations, however, showed entire cities.

The *West Shore* also issued several larger lithographs of cities as supplements. The imprint of

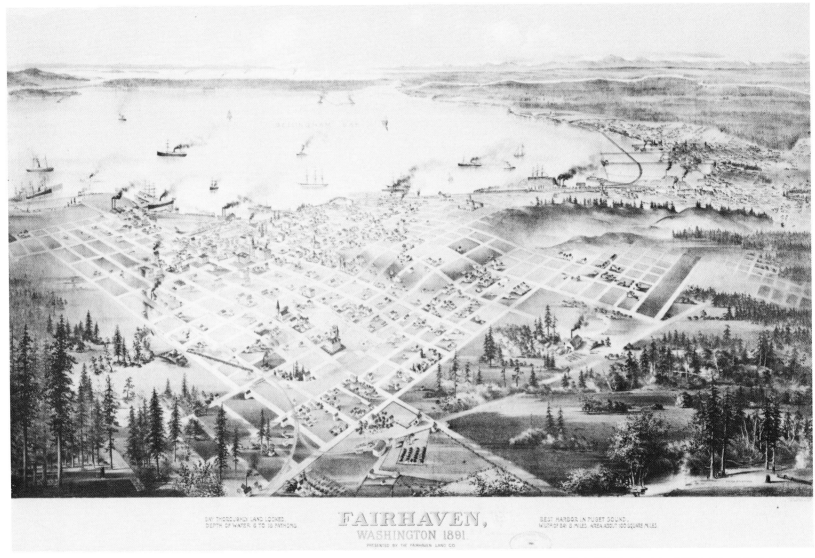

BAY THOROUGHLY LAND LOCKED.
DEPTH OF WATER 6 TO 18 FATHOMS

FAIRHAVEN,
WASHINGTON 1891.
PRESENTED BY THE FAIRHAVEN LAND CO.

BEST HARBOR IN PUGET SOUND.
WIDTH OF BAY 3 MILES. AREA ABOUT 100 SQUARE MILES.

Figure 35. Fairhaven, Washington (now part of Bellingham, Washington), 1891.   (State Historical Society of Wisconsin, Madison, Wisconsin)

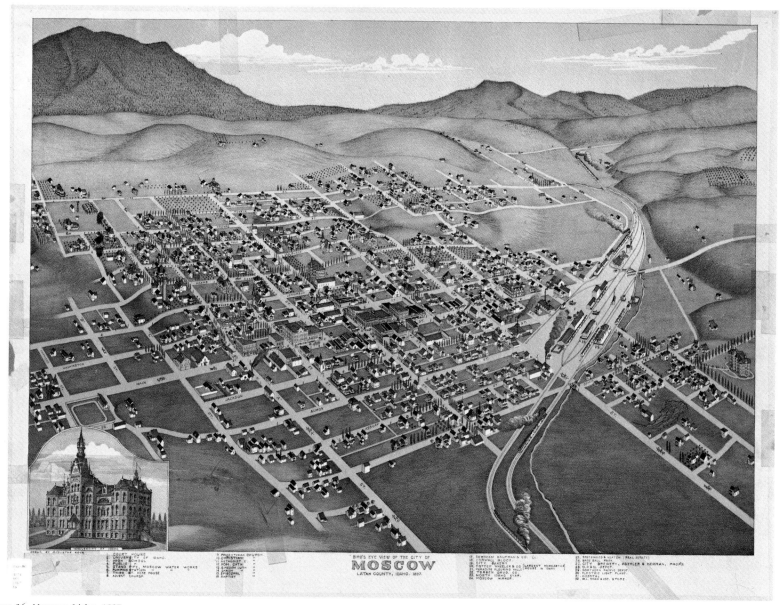

Figure 36. Moscow, Idaho, 1897.

LaGrande, Oregon, for example, identifies its source and purpose. The Roseburg, Oregon, print, published the previous year (Figure 38), carried no such designation, but it, too, was used to increase sales and circulation of the journal. Although most copies of these large supplements were folded and bound with the magazine, apparently some were available separately. A full-scale study of the *West Shore*'s pictorial activities awaits some scholar's attention. [31]

Occasionally some newspapers published city views as supplements. For instance, an unusual sectioned print distributed by the Portland *Morning Oregonian* shows drawings of Albany, Oregon City, Salem, and Eugene. More typical was the large bird's-eye view reproduced in Figure 39. Distributed by the *Colonist* of Victoria, British Columbia, this unsigned lithograph must have been an effective means of promoting subscriptions to its sponsoring newspaper.

Until recently, historians of American art have paid little attention to these views. Curators in many museums often seem almost embarrassed at having such prints in their collections. Their nineteenth-century owners, however, had different attitudes and proudly hung city views on walls of their drawing rooms and business offices. Evidence of this practice comes from lithographs in period frames or those bearing unmistakable signs of having once been so preserved. The tell-tale clue is the pattern of widely spaced vertical stains resulting from exposure to pollutants entering the slits between the slabs of wood used in old frames as backing for the prints.

Many architectural and urban historians exhibit the same lack of interest as the art curators. When they use a nineteenth-century urban lithograph to illustrate a book or article, it is usually selected only for decorative purposes, not as historical evidence to supplement findings or arguments derived from other sources. Even urban geographers, who make use of maps and plans of many types, rarely use views in their research.

Specialists in historic preservation are only beginning to employ these lithographs in researching the appearance and style of buildings in their communities. They will find a splendid archive of architectural details in the vignettes included on lithographs produced by Kuchel & Dresel, Pierce, and on others as well. They need not despair if a building that interests them is not the subject of a vignette. Close examination of the main view may reveal the desired information. Viewmakers differed in their attention to such matters. E. S. Moore's lithograph of Ashland, Oregon (Figure 32), has an almost photographic quality in its rendering of larger buildings, while Glover's depiction of Olympia a decade earlier (Figure 14) is more diagrammatic but potentially helpful nonetheless.

At a different scale, lithographs can be used to trace expansion and changes in the character of a single city. Like time-lapse photography of a flower coming into blossom, a succession of drawings at intervals of several years helps us perceive and appreciate patterns of growth and trends in development that might otherwise be overlooked. Portland and Seattle provide the best

Figure 38. *Roseburg, Oregon, [1888]. Oregon Historical Society, Portland, Oregon) Catalog Number 67*

Figure 39. *Victoria, British Columbia, 1889. (Amon Carter Museum of Western Art, Fort Worth, Texas) Catalog Number 11*

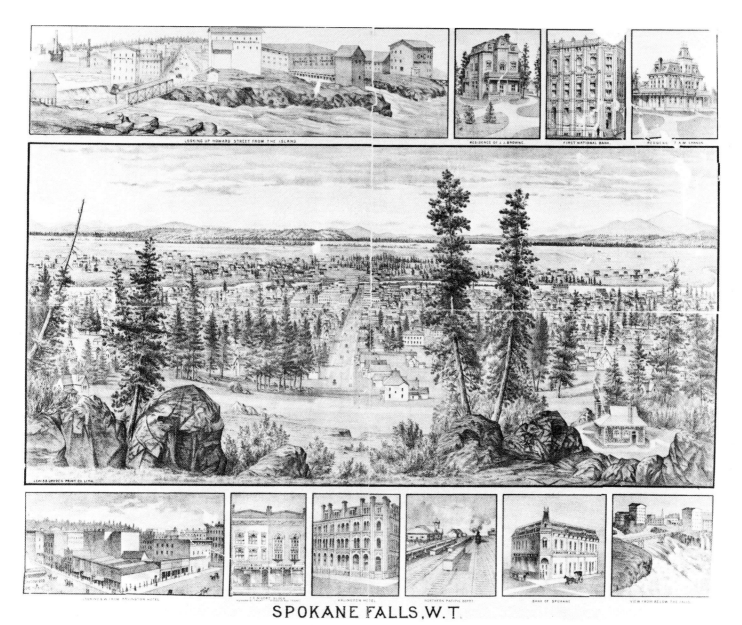

Figure 37. Spokane, Washington [1888].

ROSEBURG, OREGON.
1888

Figure 38. Roseburg, Oregon, 1888.

(Oregon Historical Society, Portland, Oregon)

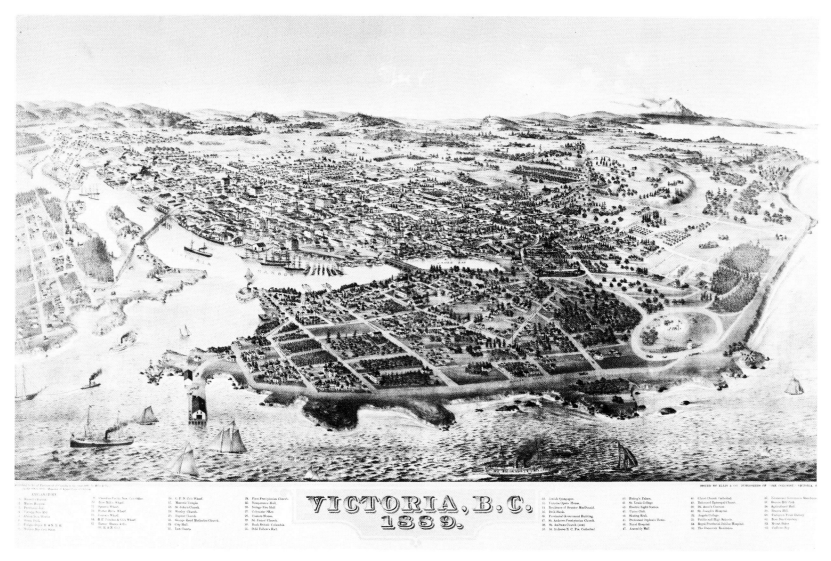

Figure 39. Victoria, British Columbia, 1889.

(Amon Carter Museum of Western Art, Fort Worth, Texas)

52

examples in the region because their size and importance led many artists and publishers to prepare lithographs of them over the years. However, there are many other places where at least three lithographic views exist. They include Astoria, Boise, Salem, Spokane, Tacoma, The Dalles, Walla Walla, as well as Victoria and Vancouver, British Columbia.[32]

Portland's lithographic view history began in 1858, when Kuchel & Dresel made the city the subject of their large and impressive drawing (Figure 40). Because they chose to depict the city from the ground level, we can see with some clarity the elevations of the major buildings along the Willamette River. Yet the print provides no information about the arrangement of the city's streets or how much of the site was occupied. The same is true of Grafton Brown's view of a few years later (Figure 22).

The first bird's-eye perspective of Portland was published in 1870 by the enterprising photographer, P. F. Castleman, who then worked in Eugene. Grafton Brown printed this view (Figure 41) at his San Francisco shop from a drawing done by C. B. Talbot. The artist used a strange perspective, but his work provides an immediate grasp of Portland's urban pattern as it had expanded in twenty-five years from its original grid two blocks wide and eight blocks long near the water's edge. Several additions provided for the city's growing population. One of these developments, platted by Daniel Lownsdale in 1848, included a novel feature: the strip of open, park blocks parallel to the river and ten blocks inland. These blocks are clearly shown in Talbot's view.[33]

In 1879 Glover published his delineation of the expanding community as viewed from the opposite direction (Figure 42). The Willamette River and Portland's suburbs on the opposite bank can be seen in the background. Some of the blocks in the Lownsdale park strip evidently proved too tempting during the decade of substantial growth and had been occupied by buildings. The port facilities that accounted for much of Portland's prosperity occupy most of the extended waterfront.

When Bruce Wellington Pierce drew the city in 1890 (Figure 7), its population was nearing 50,000. As the editor of America's leading travel guide then wrote: "The streets...are wide, regularly laid out, well paved and well lighted. The buildings of the business thoroughfares would do credit to any city, and the same may be said of many of the churches, the post office, the custom-house, and other public edifices, as well as private residences." Portland thus displayed, as the writer asserted, "all the features of a flourishing modern city."[34]

Those features included what seems to us a contemporary element of the urban scene: leapfrog sprawl. An anonymous view of 1890, printed by W. W. Elliott and probably published by a real estate developer, shows this aspect of the city's condition (Figure 43). The artist looked north at Portland and, beyond, to Vancouver, Washington, and Mt. St. Helens. He focused his attention, however, on the scattered subdivisions in the foreground. This pattern characterizes urban growth in our own era, but the view provides convincing

Figure 40. *Portland, Oregon, 1858. (Amon Carter Museum of Western Art, Fort Worth, Texas) Catalog Number 53*

Figure 41. *Portland, Oregon, 1870. (Oregon Historical Society, Portland, Oregon) Catalog Number 55*

Figure 42. *Portland, Oregon, 1879. (Geography and Map Division, Library of Congress) Catalog Number 56*

Figure 43. *Portland, Oregon, 1890. (Oregon Historical Society, Portland, Oregon) Catalog Number 62*

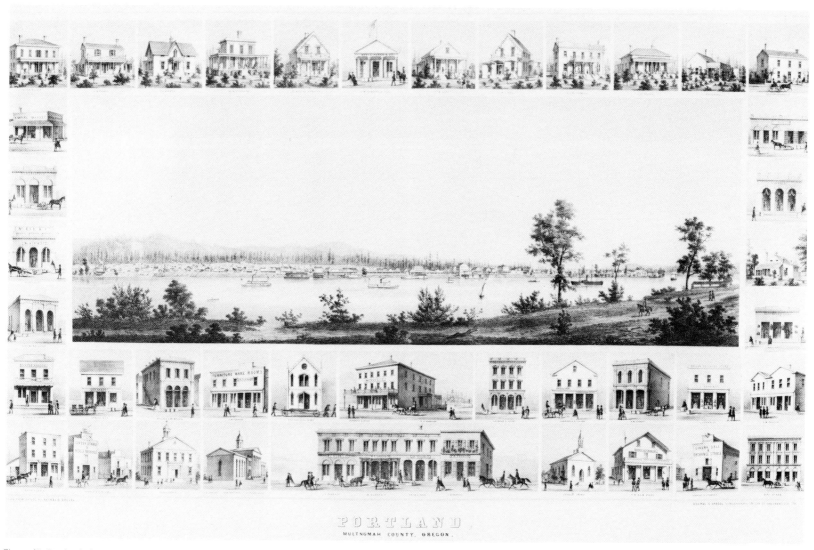

Figure 40. Portland, Oregon, 1858.

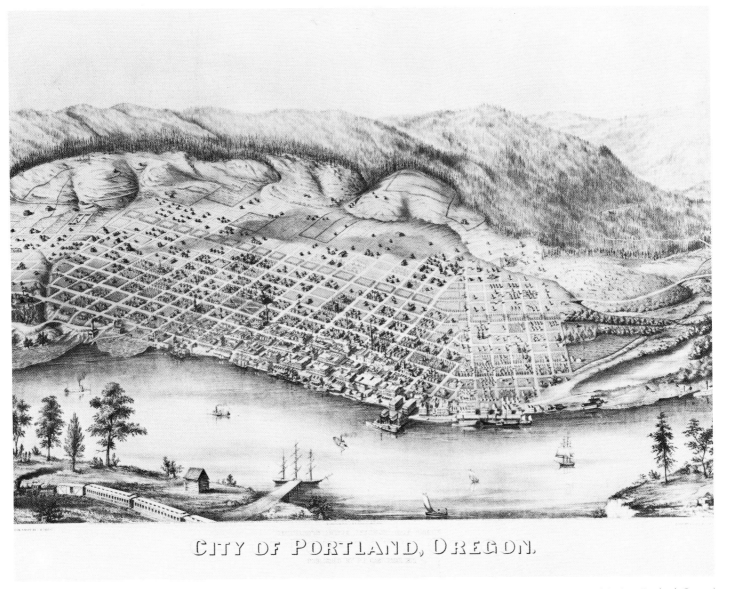

CITY OF PORTLAND, OREGON.

Figure 41. Portland, Oregon, 1870.

(Oregon Historical Society, Portland, Oregon)

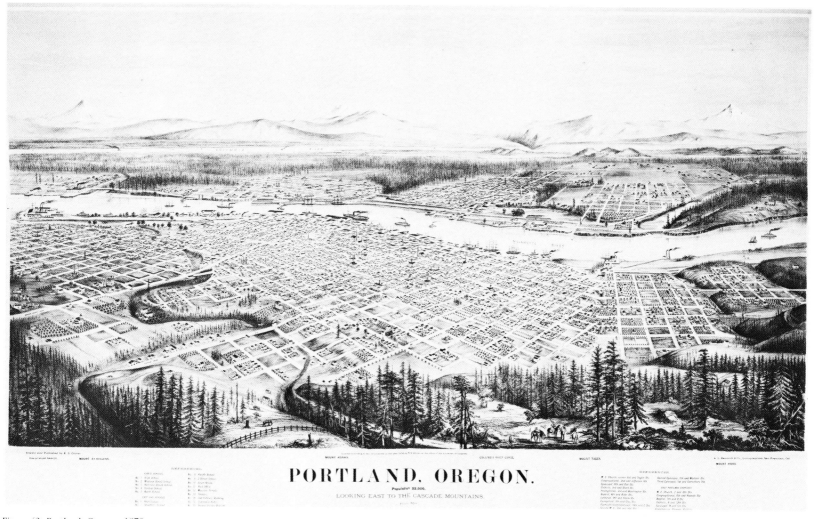

PORTLAND, OREGON.

Population 22,000.

LOOKING EAST TO THE CASCADE MOUNTAINS.

Figure 42. Portland, Oregon, 1879.

(Geography and Map Division, Library of Congress)

evidence that it is far from new.

Elliott also drew and printed another bird's-eye perspective about 1890 showing Portland's setting against the background of the entire Willamette Valley (Figure 44). On this huge print are the locations of such places as Oregon City, Salem, Eugene, and Corvallis, as well as many smaller towns dotting the banks of the river south of the metropolis. Doubtless this print was used for advertising and promotional purposes.

One of the last of Portland's lithographic city views made its appearance in 1904 (Figure 45). Its large vignette at the bottom shows the buildings and grounds of the Lewis and Clark Centennial Exposition, scheduled to open the following year. In addition to its value in portraying building design, the view extends the graphic documentation of the city's expansion into the early years of the twentieth century. It was for this lithograph that the finished drawing illustrated in Figure 16 was prepared. Comparisons of the two provide examples of changes in the

techniques of lithographic printing. For the vignettes, the printer used photographs and transferred their images to the printing surface as halftone illustrations. Probably the depiction of the city itself was also photographed and a line negative of it used to complete the printing surface— almost certainly by that time a zinc plate instead of a lithographic stone.

Seattle's growth and expansion can be traced in a similar fashion using a series of views beginning with the print by Eli S. Glover in 1878 (Figure 46). Less than twenty-five years before Glover published his drawing, one of Seattle's early residents described the place as consisting of ''but one street built on, and that but thinly, with nothing to mark the different lots, the sides and middle of the street all alike, stumpy, with miserable Indian shanties scattered all about....''[35]

Although Glover's view of Portland in 1879 (Figure 42) clearly shows that it was a far more sophisticated city, Seattle nonetheless had cast off its frontier costume. Its residents could point to many improvements,

including the university received as a consolation prize when the community lost its fight to be named the territorial capital. This educational structure, standing apart from the business district, was the largest building in town. It can be seen at the center of Glover's view, although the artist concentrated his attention on the docks and warehouses in the foreground.

Henry Wellge adopted almost the identical viewpoint for his lithograph of 1884 (Figure 47).[36] It was the year after Seattle gained a connection to the Northern Pacific Railroad via a branch line, which stimulated the development of the city's business and industry. By the time this view appeared, Seattle had pulled even with its great Puget Sound rival, Tacoma, and, as a local historian noted shortly thereafter, had ''built warehouses, graded streets, planned the erection of a big hotel, and a pretentious opera house,'' and ''was in the midst of its transition from a frontier town to a great commercial city.''[37]

Also in 1884, the *West Shore* published a view of Seattle showing the town as the artist looked

Figure 44. *Portland, Oregon, circa 1890. (Oregon Historical Society, Portland, Oregon) Catalog Number 63*

Figure 45. *Portland, Oregon, 1904. (Oregon Historical Society, Portland, Oregon) Catalog Number 65*

Figure 46. *Seattle, Washington, 1878. (Bancroft Library, University of California, Berkeley, California) Catalog Number 94*

Figure 47. *Seattle, Washington, 1884. (Historical Society of Seattle and King County, Museum of History and Industry, Seattle, Washington) Catalog Number 96*

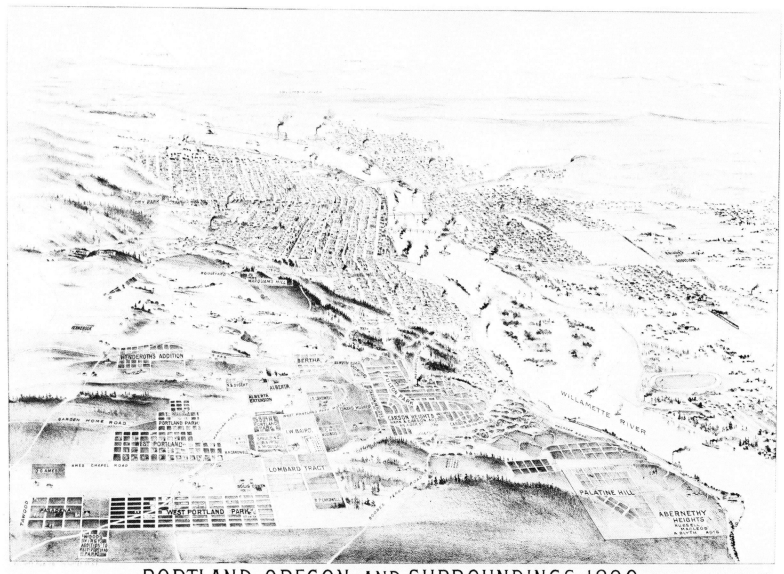

PORTLAND, OREGON; AND SURROUNDINGS. 1890.
LOOKING NORTH.

Figure 43. Portland, Oregon, 1890.

PORTLAND'S WILLAMETTE-COLUMBIA PENINSULA. PORTLAND, OR.

Figure 44. Portland, Oregon, circa 1890.

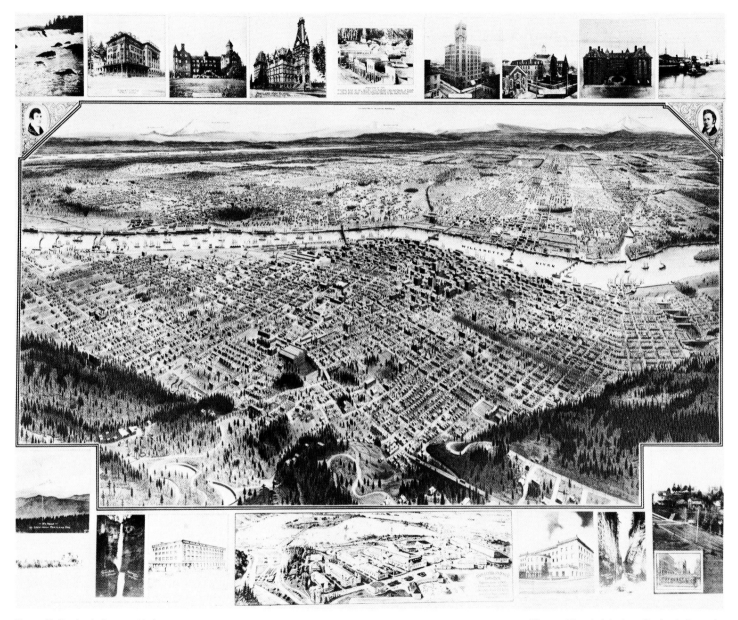

Figure 45. Portland, Oregon, 1904.

Figure 46. Seattle, Washington, 1878.

(Bancroft Library, University of California, Berkeley, California)

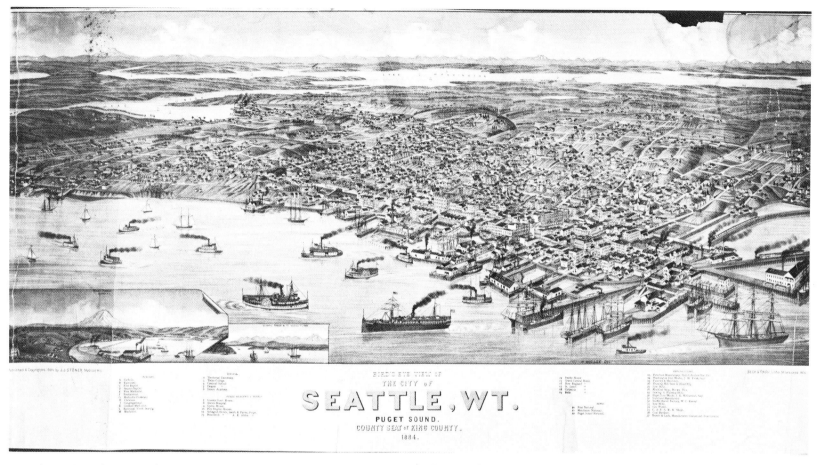

Figure 47. Seattle, Washington, 1884.

(Historical Society of Seattle and King County, Museum of History and Industry, Seattle, Washington)

62

down Front Street to the south. This lithograph (Figure 49) provides revealingly detailed information about the buildings in the foreground. It also conveys something of the character of Seattle's rugged topography and the majestic beauty of Mount Rainier in the distance.

Five years later the Elliott Publishing Company produced another protrait of Seattle (Figure 48). The artist again looked down on the city from a point above the harbor and business district. This drawing is important as the first city view of Seattle to include vignettes, and the one at the upper left is highly unusual. It shows the building occupied by Toklas, Singerman & Co., wholesale and retail drygoods merchants. The front facade is drawn in normal fashion, but the artist left the side of the building open like a dollhouse so that the interior can be seen.

Finally, this sequence of views ends with Augustus Koch's large print of 1891 (Figure 50). Koch imagined himself at a higher altitude than any of his predecessors, and he also selected a much steeper angle from which to display the scene. The result is almost map-like, with every street clearly evident. This heightened perspective permitted Koch to show development along the shores of Lake Union and Lake Washington far better than did earlier viewmakers.

Koch also makes it easier to appreciate Seattle's success in achieving the rail connections its business leaders had long desired. In the year the view was published the Great Northern Railroad designated the city as its western terminus, and the Northern Pacific, Tacoma's reason for existence, had begun to route much of its traffic through Seattle. Koch's drawing shows several rail lines that served the city, as well as their extensions from the shoreline across the harbor on causeways connecting new factories with older industrial districts.

Lithographic city views can thus be examined and analyzed in many ways and for a variety of purposes. Not everyone will wish to put them to scholarly use. Certainly they can be enjoyed for their obvious antiquarian appeal and compelling charm, for these prints reach across the years to clasp us in a nostalgic embrace. Modern owners can delight in them as wall decorations, as did their first purchasers who hung them in offices and parlors.

Whether scholar or not, we can with the aid of these views take ourselves back in time to the early years of the towns and cities in the Pacific Northwest and in our imagination approach their outskirts, visit their neighborhoods, walk their streets, admire their buildings, and appreciate the richness and variety of the urban scene in this region a century or more ago.

Figure 48. *Seattle, Washington, 1889. (Bancroft Library, University of California, Berkeley, California)*
Catalog Number 98

Figure 49. *Seattle, Washington, 1884. (Amon Carter Museum of Western Art, Fort Worth, Texas)*
Catalog Number 97

Figure 50. *Seattle, Washington, 1891. (Bancroft Library, University of California, Berkeley, California)*
Catalog Number 100

Figure 48. Seattle, Washington, 1889.

Figure 49. Seattle, Washington, 1884.

N.T. 1884

PUBLISHED By THE WEST SHORE. PORTLAND.

(Amon Carter Museum of Western Art, Fort Worth, Texas)

66

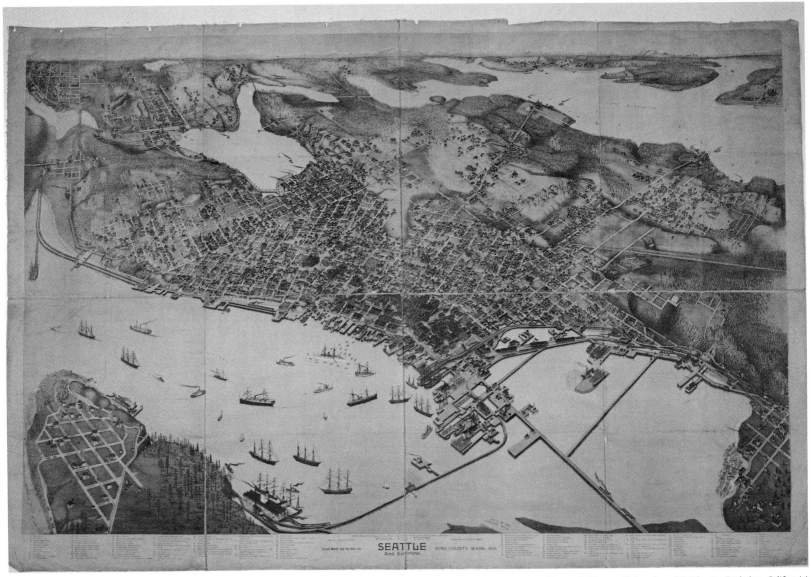

Figure 50. Seattle, Washington, 1891.

Notes

NOTES

1. In this respect the Pacific Northwest was typical of the frontiers of the entire Trans-Mississippi West. For a treatment of Western urbanization focusing on the creation of towns and cities, see John W. Reps, *Cities of the American West: A History of Frontier Urban Planning* (Princeton, New Jersey, 1979). A more compact review of the topic is found in Reps, *The Forgotten Frontier: Urban Planning in the American West Before 1890* (Columbia, Missouri, 1981). Both books cite relevant literature and bibliographies. The first volume devotes a long chapter to the Pacific Northwest.

2. This essay is a revised and expanded version of my Pettyjohn Lecture delivered at Washington State University on March 23, 1983. It is based on research done over a six-year period, most of it supported generously by a grant from the National Endowment for the Humanities. The results of that study appear in John W. Reps, *Views and Viewmakers of Urban America: Lithographs of Cities in the United States and Canada with Notes on the Artists and Publishers and a Union Catalog of Their Work, 1825-1925* (Columbia, Missouri: University of Missouri Press, 1984). Many subjects that are only touched on in this essay are dealt with there at length. However, for this book I have selected illustrations that—with a few exceptions—do not appear in that larger work.

3. Further analysis of the Cheney view could provide additional insights into this community. For example, since all the blocks appear to be the same size, an index of building coverage could be obtained by plotting the outlines of all structures and measuring or estimating the percentage of the block area they represent. Dwellings can generally be distinguished from commercial buildings, and by plotting their number in each block it would be possible to derive an approximate measure of family density by blocks throughout the town. One might also plot on separate overlays the one-story houses and the two-story houses as a rough indication of segregation by wealth.

4. This false perspective may offend artistic purists, but its use makes the views far more valuable for the kind of analysis useful to historians, geographers, and others concerned with study-ing details of individual buildings and their surroundings. Each view artist had his favorite perspective system, and those who have looked at hundreds of these prints can usually identify the artist after a quick glance, even from a distance.

5. In 1868 the Union Pacific Railroad subsidized the publication of W. Delavan's panorama showing the rail route to San Francisco. See the Omaha, Nebraska, *Weekly Republican,* August 5, 1868. Research in newspapers of the Pacific Northwest for contemporary notices concerning city views may provide supporting evidence for what I have suggested here.

6. Seattle *Post-Intelligencer,* July 15, 1884, p. 2, col. 2. See Figure 47 for this view.

7. Victoria *Colonist,* October 16, 1878, p. 3.

8. The ways in which artists, publishers, and agents promoted sales of views and how they found other sources of income are thoroughly explored in several chapters of Reps, *Views and Viewmakers of Urban America.*

9. A reproduction of the view of Constantinople from this book can be found as Figure 1, p. 4, in John W. Reps, *Cities on Stone: Nineteenth Century Lithographic Images of the Urban West* (Fort Worth, Texas, 1976).

10. There were many editions of Munster's book, testifying to its popularity. For a reproduction of his view of Florence, see Figure 2, p. 7, in ibid.

11. For the view of Moscow in this volume, see the reproduction in ibid., Figure 3, p. 9.

12. Speed used city views or plan-views (combining a map with perspectives of individual buildings) as insets on his maps of British counties. His map of the Welsh county of Flintshire with an inset of Flint is in ibid., Figure 4, p. 12. For a study of Speed's town plans and the sources he used in preparing them, see R. A. Skelton, "Tudor Town Plans in John Speed's *Theatre,"* *Archaeological Journal* 108 (1952): 109-120.

13. In addition to entries in the usual biographical dictionaries, useful material on these artists and their work can be found in A. Hyatt Mayor, "Aquatint Views of our Infant Cities," *Antiques* 88 (September 1964): 314-18; Donald A. Shelley, "William Guy Wall and his Watercolors for the Historical *Hudson River Portfolio*," *New-York Historical Society Quarterly* 21 (January 1947): 24-45; Frank Weitenkampf, "John Hill and American Landscapes in Aquatint," *American Collector,* 17 (July 1948): 6-8; Richard J. Koke, "John Hill (1770-1850), Master of Aquatint," *New-York Historical Society Quarterly* 43 (January 1959): 51-117; and Koke, *A Checklist of the American Engravings of John Hill* (1770-1850) (New York, 1961).

14. Cadwallader Colden, *Memoir...Presented...at the Celebration of the New York Canals* (New York, 1825). Despite the date on the title page, the illustrations were probably printed in 1826, the date on the attached Appendix in which they appear. They were printed at the New York City lithographic press of Anthony Imbert.

15. *United States Literary Gazette* 4 (June 15, 1826): 224-27.

16. Virtually all aspects of lithography were foreseen and described by its inventor, Alois Senefelder, in his treatise published in German and French in 1818. An English translation appeared the following year. See Alois Senefelder, *A Complete Course of Lithography* . . . (London, 1819). A modern reprint with an Introduction by A. Hyatt Mayor and a supplement of 31 plates from the first German and French editions was issued in 1977 by Da Capo Press of New York. See also J. Luther Ringwalt ed., *American Encyclopaedia of Printing* (Philadelphia, 1871). The best single book on the history and techniques of early 19th century lithography is Michael Twyman, *Lithography, 1800-1850; The Techniques of Drawing on Stone in England and France and Their Application in Works of Topography* (London, 1970). A study of American lithography focusing on color printing by this method is Peter C. Marzio, *The Democratic Art: Pictures for a 19th-Century America* (Boston, 1979).

17. One example of this technique among the lithographs of the region is the view of Hailey, Idaho, in 1884, printed in Denver.

18. Various impressions made during a single press run will vary. On at least one impression of the Portland view examined by the author at the Oregon Historical Society, yellow ink appears in places where it plainly does not belong. Whether this resulted from a minor flaw of registration during printing or was caused by an error in preparing the plate used for yellow ink could only be determined by studying representative samples of other impressions.

19. The two-stone version can be found, among other places, in the Geography and Map Division of the Library of Congress.

20. In reading scores of contemporary newpaper accounts of the activities of urban viewmakers throughout the United States and Canada, I have yet to encounter any mention of balloons. See also Arthur J. Krim, "Photographic Imagery of the American City, 1840-1860," *The Professional Geographer* 25 (May 1973): 136-39. Krim states that in 1860 one clear image of Boston was obtained from a camera in a balloon. It "was the first aerial photograph of an American city, and the only one made until the late nineteenth century. Although several aerial views of European cities were made in the 1860's and 1870's, interest by Americans in aerial photography apparently waned . . . ." Popular beliefs die hard, however, and one of them is that these Pacific Northwest views could *only* have been made by someone in the air, either a photographer or the artist himself.

21. The almost identical viewpoints used by successive artists drawing Portland and Seattle strongly suggest that they relied on earlier views to some extent.

22. For page-size reproductions of the Kuchel & Dresel views of Eugene and The Dalles, Oregon, see Reps, *Cities of the American West*, Figures 11.12 and 11.19, pp. 361 and 368.

23. Most of the Kuchel & Dresel views are known in two versions, identical except for the sheet size and the presence or absence of the vignettes.

It was not done very skillfully, for—to judge from color photographs—the green is pale and unconvincing. The lithographer of this print used another method to achieve variety. He omitted any tone on the face of many buildings, making them stand out strongly.

24. A page-size reproduction of the Astoria view can be found in Reps, *Cities of the American West*, Figure 11.10, p. 358.

25. Glenn Mason, Director, Eastern Washington State Historical Society, Spokane, has kindly provided me with many transcriptions of newspaper notices concerning Castleman's activities as a photographer and view publisher. One of these appeared in the Eugene *State Journal* for June 19, 1869 and stated that "Mr. Castleman's lithographic picture of Eugene has arrived, and he is engaged in delivering it." I have not been able to locate an impression of this view, and Mr. Mason writes that "to my knowledge (and I've kept my eyes open looking for over ten years), no copies of the 1869 litho of Eugene City are extant." Letter to the author, June 7, 1983. Earlier issues of the newspaper on February 6 and 27, 1869 mention that Castleman photographed Eugene from a nearby hill, Skinner's Butte, and intended to take the photograph to San Francisco so a lithograph could be made from it.

26. This also provides a warning that the buildings shown in the vignettes were not necessarily all of the important structures in the town. Indeed, some of them were quite small, including the residence of Philip Ritz, which is the subject of a vignette on Grafton Brown's Walla Walla view. Ritz was, however, a major civic and business leader.

27. Glover used foreground details effectively in some of his California urban lithographs, notably the view of Santa Barbara in 1877 where one can see a carriage, cattle, and two figures. This is reproduced in color in Reps, *Cities of the American West*, Plate 11, following p. 192.

28. Norfolk, Nebraska, *Daily News*, June 15, 1889; Fremont, Nebraska, *Weekly Herald*, July 4, 1889.

29. A few of Wellge's views had only short legends. One example is that of The Dalles, Oregon, which is reproduced as Figure 11.20, p. 370, in Reps, *Cities of the American West*. Only seventeen buildings are identified.

30. In the Special Collections Division, University of Washington Libraries, Seattle, there is a lithograph by Pierce of the Hotel Fairhaven. This and other Pierce material were given to the library by Lee Pierce Morris, a grandson of the artist. Dennis Andersen of Special Collections was kind enough to send a list of Pierce items in their possession, and Mr. Morris has also generously shared with me his information concerning his grandfather.

31. Several unpublished indexes to the *West Shore* exist, according to Jan Heikkala, Library Administrative Assistant, Oregon Historical Society, in a letter to the author dated February 11, 1983. Enclosed with the letter was a copy of the foreword to an index prepared in 1953 by Hazel Mills as her master's thesis in librarianship. Mr. Heikkala has a more elaborate index nearing completion. Most of my information about the magazine is based on the material in the Mills thesis.

32. I have not included Eugene, Jacksonville, and Oregon City in this list, for although the catalog entries show that each has at least three views, only two different depictions exist. The other entries represent variant states of the Kuchel & Dresel views, differing only in the presence or absence of border vignettes.

33. Talbot seems to have used a vanishing point at the upper right several miles beyond the horizon, for the streets leading in that direction barely converge. For the streets running parallel to the river Talbot appears to have used no vanishing point whatsoever. In fact, his streets diverge slightly with distance, creating an effect that is unsettling if looked at intently.

34. *Appletons' General Guide to the United States and Canada* (New York, 1892), p. 485.

35. Letter from Mrs. David E. Blaine to her mother, August, 1854, as quoted in Clarence B. Bagley, *History of Seattle from the Earliest Settlement to the Present Time* (Chicago, 1916) I:36.

36. An announcement concerning the view in the Seattle *Post-Intelligencer* for July 15, 1884, p. 2, col. 2, tells us something about the time the artist required to complete his drawing, the price at which the lithograph sold, and the way in which these prints were described to potential customers: "H. Wellge, an artist who has been here during the past fortnight, has

completed in ink the finest view of Seattle ever taken. It is of the bird's-eye character, and shows everything for two miles up and down the bay, and out to and on Lakes Union and Washington, as also the bay in front of the town. On the bay are a large number of vessels—screw, stern and sidewheel steamers, sail vessels of all rigs and small boats. In the town are shown the streets and houses, fences, gardens and shade trees, with the timber beyond, all beautifully plain, clear and distinct. With but little difficulty every house in town can be picked out. The picture is fourteen inches wide and thirty-three inches long. It will be lithographed, printed on card board, and sold to our citizens at the rate of $2 apiece, twelve for $20, and $1 apiece for hundred.''

37. Frederic James Grant, ''Seattle: A Chapter from an Uncompleted History,'' *Magazine of Western History* 11 (April 1890): 641.

Catalog of Lithographic
Views of the Pacific Northwest

CATALOG OF LITHOGRAPHIC
VIEWS OF THE PACIFIC NORTHWEST

The entries that follow record the separately issued lithographic city views of British Columbia, Oregon, Idaho, and Washington, as well as those portions of Montana west of the Continental Divide. These were identified during the compilation of a national union catalog of such prints. Other views doubtless exist, but since major national collections, those of state historical societies, and many other institutions in the region have been searched or queried, this catalog is reasonably complete.

Persons using it should understand how to interpret the entries. The paragraphs that follow explain what information is provided under each of the eleven subheadings used to describe and analyze each view. Entries appear in alphabetical order by province or state and then by city. Where more than one view of a city exists, entries are arranged chronologically, beginning with the earliest. Each main entry has been assigned a number according to the order in which it appears.

PLACE. This is the name of the town or city depicted. If more than one town or city is named in the title, the place whose name appears first is used for the main entry. Cross-reference listings are used for the other names.

DATE. This is the date of publication of the view, usually that appearing in the title or copyright claim. A date in brackets indicates that the print is undated but that its time of publication has been otherwise established. An approximate date is preceded by "circa."

TITLE. The title is given as it appears on the print, including any errors in spelling or punctuation. However, no attempt has been made to duplicate the original use of capital or lower case letters.

SIZE. Vertical dimensions are given first, followed by horizontal. The first set of measurements is in inches, and the second set (in parentheses) is in centimeters. Measurements are intended to encompass all of the printed surface, including titles, legends, and borders, but not blank margins. However, some measurements come from sources that excluded titles and other material beyond the inner borders of prints.

ARTIST. The name of the artist is provided as it is signed on the print. Brackets are used to enclose the name of the artist of an unsigned print if the name is known from other sources.

LITHOGRAPHER. This name is recorded in the same manner as the artist. Lithographers put the artist's drawing on stone, but they did not often sign their names to the print. It should be noted that such phrases as "lith of" or "lith by" found on many views of this period almost always designate the printer. On some views the artist was his own lithographer. This is often indicated by some version of the phrase "From Nature and on Stone by" before the name of the artist-lithographer.

PRINTER. The name of the printer and the printer's address is recorded as it appears on the lithograph.

PUBLISHER. The name and address of the publisher is recorded in the same manner as the printer. If no publisher's name appears on the print but a copyright claimant is identified, that name is used followed by the word "copyright" in parentheses.

KEY/VIGNETTES/MISC. Many prints include a key or legend. Where this has numbers or letters identifying places shown on the view, the inclusive numbers or letters are noted. For example, "Refs. 1-12, A-D" indicates that the legend has numbered references from 1 through 12 and lettered references A through D. If only the total number of references is known, the entry would read "16 references." An entry reading "12 vignettes" means that in addition to the principal view there are twelve border or inset views of details of the place. Other entries under this heading include such notes as "unnumbered business directory" and "description," the latter being any descriptive text appearing within or outside the borders of the view.

LOCATIONS. These are museums, libraries, or historical societies known to own at least one impression of the view. Codes are used to save space. A list of these codes follows this note. Institutions holding less than three views are identified in uncoded fashion. Ownership of an image other than an original lithograph is indicated by the use of "(photo)" or "(facsimile)" after the institution identification.

CATALOGS/CHECKLISTS. Under this heading the entry lists published collection or exhibition catalogs, checklists, and similar published sources that identify (and perhaps illustrate) the view. Abbreviated or coded references are used. Full citations of each source can be found at the end of the catalog.

Institutions Identified in Catalog Entries Holding Original Impressions of Lithographic Views

LOCATION CODE	INSTITUTION
ACMW-FW	Amon Carter Museum of Western Art, Fort Worth, Texas
BPL-R	Rare Book Department, Boston Public Library, Boston, Massachusetts
CHS-C	Chicago Historical Society, Chicago, Illinois
EWHS-S	Eastern Washington State Historical Society, Spokane, Washington
HEHL	Henry E. Huntington Library, San Marino, California
ISHS-B	Idaho State Historical Society, Boise, Idaho
LC-M	Geography and Map Division, Library of Congress, Washington, D.C.
LCM-E	Lane County Museum, Eugene, Oregon
LC-P	Prints and Photographs Division, Library of Congress, Washington, D.C.
MHS-H	Montana Historical Society, Helena, Montana
MM-NN	Mariners Museum, Newport News, Virginia
MTLB-T	Metropolitan Toronto Library Board, Toronto, Ontario
NHM-LA	Natural History Museum, Los Angeles County, Los Angeles, California
NL-C	Newberry Library, Chicago, Illinois
NYH-NY	The New-York Historical Society, New York, New York
NYP-S	Stokes Collection, New York Public Library, New York, New York
OHS-P	Oregon Historical Society, Portland, Oregon
OUL-E	University of Oregon Library, Eugene, Oregon
PABC-V	Provincial Archives of British Columbia, Victoria, British Columbia

LOCATION CODE	INSTITUTION
PAC	Map Division, Public Archives of Canada, Ottawa, Ontario
PAC-P	Picture Division, Public Archives of Canada, Ottawa, Ontario
PLW-WW	Penrose Memorial Library, Whitman College, Walla Walla, Washington
PUL-P	Princeton University Library, Princeton, New Jersey
ROM	Royal Ontario Museum, Canadiana Department Collection, Toronto, Ontario
RU-NB	Special Collections Department, Alexander Library, Rutgers University, New Brunswick, New Jersey
SHS-S	Seattle Historical Society, Seattle, Washington
SOHS-J	Southern Oregon Historical Society, Jacksonville, Oregon
UCBL-B	Bancroft Library, University of California, Berkeley, California
UML-M	Mansfield Library, University of Montana, Missoula, Montana
UWL-S	Special Collections, University of Washington Libraries, Seattle, Washington
WHPL-D	Western History Department, Denver Public Library, Denver, Colorado
WHS-M	Wisconsin Historical Society, Madison, Wisconsin
WSHS-T	Washington State Historical Society, Tacoma, Washington

1. **New Westminster, British Columbia**
Date: 1890
Title: New Westminster, B.C. 1890
Size:
Artist:
Lithographer:
Publisher:
Key/Vignettes/Misc: References; 30 vignettes
Locations: University of British Columbia Library, Vancouver, British
   Columbia (photo)
Catalogs/Checklists: Reps, VVUA, 28

2. **North Vancouver, British Columbia**
Date: 1907
Title: Bird's Eye View of the City of North Vancouver, B.C. From the
   Harbor . . . 1907.
Size: 14 15/16 × 17 13/16 inches (38 × 45.4 cm.)
Artist: C. H. Rawson
Lithographer:
Publisher: Irwin & Billings Co. Ltd.
Key/Vignettes/Misc: One blank vignette
Locations: PAC
Catalogs/Checklists: PAC H3/640-North Vancouver-1907; Reps, VVUA, 29

3. **Vancouver, British Columbia**
Date: 1890
Title: Vancouver, B.C. 1890.
Size: 24 1/16 × 37 5/16 inches (61.2 × 95 cm.)
Artist:
Lithographer: F. W.
Printer: Elliott Pub. Co. 120 Sutter St., S. F.
Publisher: Vancouver Daily and Weekly World Publishing Co.
Key/Vignettes/Misc: References 1-71; 41 vignettes
Locations: PAC; PABC-V
Catalogs/Checklists: PAC (1976); PAC; Reps, VVUA, 30

4. **Vancouver, British Columbia**
Date: 1898
Title: Panoramic View of the City of Vancouver, British Columbia 1898
Size: 27 7/8 × 40 1/8 inches (71 × 102 cm.)
Artist: J.[ohn] C.[ampbell] McLagan
Lithographer:
Printer: Toronto Lithographing Co., Ltd.
Publisher: Vancouver World Printing and Publishing Company
Key/Vignettes/Misc: 160 References; 1 vignette
Locations: PAC; PABC-V; LC-M (facsimile)
Catalogs/Checklists: PAC (1976); PAC H1/640-Vancouver-1898; LC-M,
   1074.4; Reps, VVUA, 31

5. **Vancouver, British Columbia**
Date: 1907
Title: Birds Eye View of Vancouver B.C.
Size: 15 5/16 × 21 1/4 inches (39 × 54 cm.)
Artist: C. H. Rawson
Lithographer:

Printer: Angell Eng. Co.
Publisher: Morden & Thornton (copyright)
Key/Vignettes/Misc:
Locations: PAC
Catalogs/Checklists: PAC H12/640-Vancouver-1907; Reps, VVUA, 32

6. **Vancouver, British Columbia**
Date: 1908
Title: City of Vancouver B.C. Canada. 1908
Size: 12 3/8 × 23 1/8 inches (31.5 × 59 cm.)
Artist: C. M. Arndt
Lithographer:
Printer: Dominion-Ill Co., Ltd, Vancouver
Publisher: Vancouver Tourist Association
Key/Vignettes/Misc:
Locations: PAC; PABC-V
Catalogs/Checklists: PAC H12/640-Vancouver-1908; Reps, VVUA, 33

7. **Victoria, British Columbia**
Date: 1860
Title: View of Victoria, Vancouver Island
Size: 9 7/8 × 34 5/16 inches (25.1 × 87.2 cm.)
Artist: H. O. Tiedemann
Lithographer: T. Picken
Printer: Day & Son
Publisher: Day & Son, London
Key/Vignettes/Misc: 14 unnumbered references below places identified
Locations: UCBL-B; LC-M; PAC; PABC-V; ROM; NYP-S; MTLB-T; University
   of British Columbia Library, Vancouver, British Columbia; PAC-P
Catalogs/Checklists: LC-M, 1075; PAC H3/640-Victoria-1860; Robertson,
   number 5; Stokes P. 1859—H-31; Reps, VVUA, 34

8. **Victoria, British Columbia**
Date: [1860?]
Title: View of Victoria
Size: 4 1/4 × 7 1/8 inches (10.7 × 18.2 cm.)
Artist:
Lithographer:
Printer: Clayton & Co., Lith. 17, Bouverie St.
Publisher:
Key/Vignettes/Misc:
Locations: PAC-P
Catalogs/Checklists: Reps, VVUA, 35

9. **Victoria, British Columbia**
Date: 1878
Title: Bird's-Eye View of Victoria, Vancouver Island, B.C. 1878.
Size: 21 1/8 × 32 5/16 inches (53.6 × 82.2 cm.)
Artist: E. S. Glover
Lithographer:
Printer: A. L. Bancroft & Co., San Francisco
Publisher: M. W. Waitt & Co., Victoria, B.C.
Key/Vignettes/Misc: References 1-29
Locations: LC-M; UCBL-B; PAC; PABC-V; MTLB-T; PAC-P

Catalogs/Checklists: LC-M, 1076; PAC (1976); PAC V1/640-Victoria-1878; Robertson, Number 25; Reps, VVUA, 36

10. **Victoria, British Columbia**
Date: 1884
Title: Victoria, B.C. and Vicinity 1884.
Size: 22 3/4 × 31 13/16 inches (58 × 81 cm.)
Artist: L. Samuel
Lithographer:
Printer: The West Shore
Publisher: J. B. Ferguson & Co., Victoria
Key/Vignettes/Misc: 9 views on sheet
Locations: LC-M; PABC-V
Catalogs/Checklists: LC-M, 1076.1; Reps, VVUA, 37

11. **Victoria, British Columbia**
Date: 1889
Title: Victoria, B.C. 1889
Size: 25 × 39 7/16 inches (63.6 × 100.3 cm.)
Artist: R. H.
Lithographer:
Printer:
Publisher: Ellis & Co., Victoria, B.C.
Key/Vignettes/Misc: References 1-63
Locations: LC-M; UCBL-B; ACMW-FW; UWL-S; PABC-V; MTLB-T; Victoria, B.C., City Archives; PAC-P
Catalogs/Checklists: LC-M, 1077; ACMW-FW 1867; PAC (1976); PAC H3/640-Victoria-1889; Reps, VVUA, 38

IDAHO

12. **Atlanta, Idaho**
Date: circa 1880
Title: Atlanta. Alturas County—Idaho.
Size: 15 7/16 × 20 1/2 inches (39.2 × 52 cm.)
Artist: E. Green
Lithographer:
Printer: Britton & Rey. S. F. Cal.
Publisher:
Key/Vignettes/Misc:
Locations: ACMW-FW
Catalogs/Checklists: ACMW-FW 1134; Reps, VVUA, 761

13. **Boise, Idaho**
Date: [1879]
Title: Boise City. Principle Business Houses and Private Residences
Size: 20 × 26 inches (50.9 × 66.2 cm.)
Artist: Charles Leopold Ostner
Lithographer:
Printer:
Publisher:
Key/Vignettes/Misc:
Locations: ISHS-B; Boise, Idaho, Public Library
Catalogs/Checklists: VVUA, 762

14. **Boise, Idaho**
Date: [1890]
Title: Bird's Eye view of Boise City, Ada County, the Capital of Idaho.
Size: 24 1/2 × 32 inches (62.4 × 81.4 cm.)
Artist: [Augustus Koch]
Lithographer:
Printer:
Publisher:
Key/Vignettes/Misc: References 1-20; 4 vignettes
Locations: Boise, Idaho, Public Library
Catalogs/Checklists: Reps, VVUA, 763

15. **Boise, Idaho**
Date: No Date
Title: View of Boise City, Idaho From the the Court House.
Size: 10 1/4 × 36 1/2 inches (26 × 92.6 cm.)
Artist: E. Green
Lithographer:
Printer: Britton & Rey, San Francisco
Publisher:
Key/Vignettes/Misc:
Locations: ACMW-FW
Catalogs/Checklists: ACMW-FW 1137; Reps, *Cities on Stone*, p. 91; Reps, VVUA, 764

16. **Custer, Idaho**
Date: 1880
Title: Custer, Idaho—1880.
Size: 15 3/16 × 22 1/2 inches (38.5 × 57.1 cm.)
Artist: G. W. Hall
Lithographer:
Printer: Omaha Lithographing Co. Omaha, Neb.
Publisher:
Key/Vignettes/Misc:
Locations: ACMW-FW; ISHS-B
Catalogs/Checklists: Reps, VVUA, 765

17. **Hailey, Idaho**
Date: 1884
Title: Wood River Valley with Hailey in the Foreground, 1884
Size: 14 1/2 × 22 1/8 inches (36.8 × 56.3 cm.)
Artist:
Lithographer:
Printer: The Collier & Cleaveland Lith. Co., Denver, Col.
Publisher: A. E. Browning, Salt Lake City, Utah (copyright)
Key/Vignettes/Misc: References 1-25, A-Z; Description
Locations: Blaine County Historical Museum, Hailey, Idaho; LC-M
Catalogs/Checklists: LC-M, 134; Reps, VVUA, 766

18. **Moscow, Idaho**
Date: 1887
Title: Bird's Eye View of the City of Moscow, Latah County, Idaho. 1887
Size: 24 × 32 inches (61.1 × 81.4 cm.)
Artist: Augustus Koch
Lithographer:
Printer:

Publisher:
Key/Vignettes/Misc: References 1-32; 1 vignette
Locations: University of Idaho Library, Moscow, Idaho
Catalogs/Checklists: Reps, VVUA, 767

19. **Quartzburg, Idaho**
Date: 1880
Title: Quartzburgh. Boise Co., Idaho Ty
Size: 9 1/2 × 15 inches (24.2 × 38.2 cm.)
Artist: H. Steinegger
Lithographer:
Printer: Britton & Rey, San Francisco
Publisher:
Key/Vignettes/Misc:
Locations: ISHS-B
Catalogs/Checklists: Reps, VVUA, 768

20. **Rocky Bar, Idaho**
Date: Circa 1880
Title: Rocky Bar. Alturas Co., Idaho
Size: 14 × 23 3/4 inches (35.6 × 60.5 cm.)
Artist: H. Steinegger, E. Green
Lithographer:
Printer: Britton & Rey, San Francisco
Publisher:
Key/Vignettes/Misc:
Locations: ISHS-B
Catalogs/Checklists: Reps, VVUA, 769

21. **Silver City, Idaho**
Date: Circa 1866
Title: Silver City, Owyhee, I. T.
Size: 23 × 28 1/4 inches (58.6 × 71.9 cm.)
Artist: From photographs by P. F. Castleman
Lithographer:
Printer: Grafton T. Brown & Co. Lith. 543 Clay St., San Francisco
Publisher: P. F. Castleman
Key/Vignettes/Misc: 28 vignettes
Locations: ISHS-B
Catalogs/Checklists: Reps, VVUA, 770

MONTANA

22. **Butte, Montana**
Date: 1884
Title: Bird's Eye View of Butte-City Montana County Seat of Silver Bow Co. 1884
Size: 20 × 29 inches (50.8 × 73.7 cm.)
Artist: H. Wellge
Lithographer:
Printer: Beck & Pauli, Litho. Milwaukee, Wis.
Publisher: J. J. Stoner, Madison, Wisconsin
Key/Vignettes/Misc: References 1-95; 8 vignettes
Locations: LC-M; MHS-H; ACMW-FW
Catalogs/Checklists: LC-M, 453; Reps, *Cities on Stone,* p. 91; Reps, VVUA, 2081

23. **Butte, Montana**
Date: ?
Title: Bird's Eye View of Butte City, Montana
Size: 9 (cropped) × 17 7/8 inches (22.6 × 45.5 cm.)
Artist:
Lithographer:
Printer:
Publisher:
Key/Vignettes/Misc:
Locations: UML-M
Catalogs/Checklists: Reps, VVUA, 2082

24. **Deer Lodge, Montana**
Date: [1883-1884]
Title: Bird's Eye View of Deer Lodge City. County Seat of Deer Lodge Co. Montana 1883-4
Size: 18 × 23 1/2 inches (45.8 × 59.8 cm.)
Artist:
Lithographer:
Printer: Beck & Pauli, Litho., Milwaukee
Publisher: J. J. Stoner, Madison, Wis.
Key/Vignettes/Misc: References 1-32; 1 vignette
Locations: MSH-H
Catalogs/Checklists: Reps, VVUA, 2083

25. **Kalispell, Montana**
Date: 1897
Title: Bird's Eye View of the City of Kalispell, Flathead County, Montana. 1897 Looking Southwest
Size: 21 3/4 × 27 1/4 inches (55.3 × 69.3 cm.)
Artist: Augustus Koch
Lithographer:
Printer:
Publisher:
Key/Vignettes/Misc: References 1-32
Locations: UML-M
Catalogs/Checklists: Reps, VVUA, 2091

26. **Missoula, Montana**
Date: 1884
Title: Bird's Eye View of Missoula, Mon. County Seat of Missoula County 1884.
Size: 13 1/16 × 24 1/16 inches (33.5 × 61.3 cm.)
Artist: H. Wellge
Lithographer:
Printer: Beck & Pauli, Litho. Milwaukee, Wis.
Publisher: J. J. Stoner, Madison, Wisconsin
Key/Vignettes/Misc: References 1-18; 3 vignettes; unnumbered business directory
Locations: ACMW-FW; LC-M; UML-M
Catalogs/Checklists: LC-M, 460; Reps, *Cities on Stone,* p. 94; Reps, VVUA, 2094

27. **Missoula, Montana**
Date: 1891
Title: Perspective Map of Missoula, Mont. County Seat of Missoula County.

Size: 18 1/2 × 33 inches (47 × 84 cm.)
Artist:
Lithographer:
Printer:
Publisher: American Publishing Co. Milwaukee
Key/Vignettes/Misc: 3 vignettes
Locations: LC-M; ACMW-FW; UML-M
Catalogs/Checklists: LC-M, 461; Reps, VVUA, 2095

OREGON

28. **Albany, Oregon**
Date: 1889
Title: Bird's Eye View of Albany, Linn County, Oregon 1889.
Size: 18 7/8 × 23 5/8 inches (48 × 60 cm.)
Artist:
Lithographer:
Printer: Elliott Publ. Co., San Francisco
Publisher: Albany Board of Trade
Key/Vignettes/Misc:
Locations: OUL-E
Catalogs/Checklists: Reps, VVUA, 3251

29. **Ashland, Oregon**
Date: 1884
Title: Bird's Eye View of Ashland, Jackson County, Oregon 1884. Looking
    South East. Population 1500
Size: 14 × 21 1/2 inches (35.5 × 54.5 cm.)
Artist: [Fred A. Walpole]
Lithographer:
Printer: Beck & Pauli, Milwaukee, Wis.
Publisher:
Key/Vignettes/Misc: References 1-12
Locations: SOHS-J
Catalogs/Checklists: Reps, VVUA, 3252

30. **Ashland, Oregon**
Date: 1890
Title: Bird's Eye View of Ashland, Oregon
Size: 19 1/8 × 22 5/8 inches (48.5 × 57 cm.)
Artist: E. S. Moore
Lithographer:
Printer:
Publisher:
Key/Vignettes/Misc: 5 vignettes
Locations: SOHS-J
Catalogs/Checklists: Reps, VVUA, 3253

31. **Astoria, Oregon**
Date: 1846
Title: Fort George Formerly Astoria.
Size: 8 × 12 inches (20.4 × 30.6 cm.)
Artist: [Henry James Warre]
Lithographer:
Printer:

Publisher:
Key/Vignettes/Misc:
Locations: Washington State University Libraries
Catalogs/Checklists: Spendlove, *Face of Early Canada*, p. 77; Reps, VVUA,
    3254

32. **Astoria, Oregon**
Date: [1870]
Title: Astoria Clatsop Co. Oregon. The Proposed Terminus of the North
    Pacific R. R.
Size: 14 3/16 × 22 5/16 inches (36.1 × 56.8 cm.)
Artist: Castleman and Talbot
Lithographer:
Printer: G. T. Brown & Co. Lith. 540 Clay St. S. F.
Publisher: Capt. J. G. Hustler
Key/Vignettes/Misc: 2 vignettes
Locations: UCBL-B; OHS-P
Catalogs/Checklists: Reps, VVUA, 3255

33. **Astoria, Oregon**
Date: 1887
Title: Oregon.—General View of Astoria, Looking Inland.
Size: 8 1/4 × 15 7/8 inches (21 × 40.4 cm.)
Artist:
Lithographer:
Printer: West Shore Litho. & Eng. Co. Portland, Or.
Publisher: [The *West Shore*, Portland, Oregon]
Key/Vignettes/Misc:
Locations: PUL-P
Catalogs/Checklists: Reps, VVUA, 3256

34. **Astoria, Oregon**
Date: 1887
Title: Oregon—General View of Astoria, Looking Seaward
Size: 8 1/4 × 15 7/8 inches (21 × 40.4 cm.)
Artist:
Lithographer:
Printer: West Shore Litho. & Eng Co. Portland, Or.
Publisher: [The *West Shore*, Portland, Oregon]
Key/Vignettes/Misc:
Locations: OUL-E
Catalogs/Checklists: Reps, VVUA, 3257

35. **Astoria, Oregon**
Date: 1890
Title: Stengle's View of Astoria Oregon 1890
Size: 22 3/8 × 35 7/8 inches (57 × 91.3 cm.)
Artist: [B. W.] Pierce
Lithographer:
Printer:
Publisher: J. W. Stengle (copyright)
Key/Vignettes/Misc: References 1-60; 26 vignettes
Locations: MM-NN; ACMW-FW; OUL-E; SOHS-J; Clatsop County Historical
    Museum, Astoria, Oregon; OHS-P; UCBL-B
Catalogs/Checklists: MM-NN, LP 4303; ACMW-FW, 1677; Reps, VVUA,
    3258

36. **Eugene, Oregon**
Date: 1859
Title: Eugene City, Lane County, Oregon. 1859
Size: 13 3/4 × 20 5/8 inches (34.9 × 52.3 cm.)
Artist: Kuchel & Dresel
Lithographer: Kuchel & Dresel
Printer: [Britton & Rey, San Francisco?]
Publisher: Danforth & Bro.
Key/Vignettes/Misc: 12 vignettes
Locations: ACMW-FW (Proof before tone stone); LCM-E (cropped)
Catalogs/Checklists: Reps, VVUA, 3259

37. **Eugene, Oregon**
Date: 1859
Title: Eugene City, Lane County, Oregon. 1859
Size: 7 7/8 × 14 1/8 inches (20 × 36 cm.)
Artist: Kuchel & Dresel
Lithographer: Kuchel & Dresel
Printer:
Publisher:
Key/Vignettes/Misc:
Locations: UCBL-B
Catalogs/Checklists: Reps, VVUA, 3260

38. **Eugene, Oregon**
Date: [1859?]
Title: Eugene City, Oregon
Size:
Artist: Kuchel & Dresel
Lithographer: Kuchel & Dresel
Printer: Britton & Rey
Publisher:
Key/Vignettes/Misc:
Locations:
Catalogs/Checklists: Peters, COS, p. 143; Reps, VVUA, 3261

39. **Eugene, Oregon**
Date: 1890
Title: Eugene, Oregon, 1890
Size: 24 × 32 inches (61.1 × 81.4 cm.)
Artist:
Lithographer:
Printer: Elliot Pub. Co. 120 Sutter St., S. F.
Publisher: Geo. M. Miller, Eugene, Or.
Key/Vignettes/Misc: References 1-43; 1 vignette; description
Locations: LCM-E
Catalogs/Checklists: Reps, VVUA, 3262

40. **Eugene, Oregon**
Date: [1890?]
Title: Eugene, Lane County, Oregon.
Size: 21 × 28 inches (53.4 × 71.2 cm)
Artist:
Lithographer:
Printer: Elliott Pub. Co. S. F.
Publisher: J. A. Straight & Co. . . Eugene, Or.

Key/Vignettes/Misc: References 1-35; 14 vignettes; description
Locations: LCM-E; OHS-P (photo)
Catalogs/Checklists: Reps, VVUA, 3263

41. **Grants Pass, Oregon**
Date: [1890]
Title: Birdseye View of Grants Pass, Oregon.
Size: 22 7/8 × 31 7/8 inches (58 × 81 cm.)
Artist: E. S. Moore
Lithographer:
Printer:
Publisher: Arthur Conklin, Real Estate, Loans and Investment
Key/Vignettes/Misc:
Locations: OUL-E
Catalogs/Checklists: Reps, VVUA, 3264

42. **Jacksonville, Oregon**
Date: 1856
Title: Jacksonville, Jackson County, Oregon T. 1856
Size: 15 1/2 × 21 1/2 inches (39.5 × 55 cm.)
Artist: Kuchel & Dresel
Lithographer: Kuchel & Dresel
Printer: Britton & Rey [San Francisco]
Publisher: W. W. Fowler & C. C. Beekman [Jacksonville, Ore.]
Key/Vignettes/Misc: 19 vignettes
Locations: SOHS-J; OHS-P (photo)
Catalogs/Checklists: Reps, VVUA, 3265

43. **Jacksonville, Oregon**
Date: 1856
Title: Jacksonville, O. T.
Size: 9 1/16 × 15 1/16 inches (23 × 38.3 cm.)
Artist: Kuchel & Dresel
Lithographer: Kuchel & Dresel
Printer: Britton & Rey [San Francisco]
Publisher:
Key/Vignettes/Misc:
Locations: ACMW-FW
Catalogs/Checklists: ACMW-FW, 1260; Reps, VVUA, 3266

44. **Jacksonville, Oregon**
Date: 1883
Title: Bird's Eye View of Jacksonville and the Rogue River Valley, Oregon. Looking North East. Population 1000 1883
Size: 14 × 21 1/2 inches (35.5 × 54.5 cm.)
Artist: Fred A. Walpole
Lithographer:
Printer: Beck & Pauli, Milwaukee, Wis.
Publisher: Fred A. Walpole (copyright)
Key/Vignettes/Misc: References 1-12; 1 vignette
Locations: LC-M; SOHS-J; OHS-P (facsimile); LC-P
Catalogs/Checklists: LC-M, 717; Reps, VVUA, 3267

45. **La Grande, Oregon**
Date: [1889]
Title: The Grande Ronde Valley as Seen from La Grande Oregon

Size: 13 7/8 × 20 inches (35.3 × 50.9 cm.)
Artist:
Lithographer:
Printer:
Publisher: The *West Shore* Magazine, Portland-Or.
Key/Vignettes/Misc:
Locations: OHS-P
Catalogs/Checklists: Reps, VVUA, 3268

46. **Marshfield, Oregon**
Date: 1884
Title: View of Marshfield, Coos County, Oregon
Size: 15 1/4 × 27 1/2 inches (38.8 × 70 cm.)
Artist: E. F. Cook
Lithographer:
Printer: Britton & Rey, S. F.
Publisher:
Key/Vignettes/Misc:
Locations: Coos-Curry Museum, North Bend, Oregon
Catalogs/Checklists: Reps, VVUA, 3269

47. **Oregon City, Oregon**
Date: 1846
Title: The American Village
Size: 9 13/16 × 13 1/8 inches (24.8 × 33.3 cm.)
Artist: H[enry] J.[ames] Warre
Lithographer:
Printer: Dickenson & Co., [London]
Publisher:
Key/Vignettes/Misc:
Locations: ACMW-FW; PAC-P; ROM; Washington State University Libraries, Pullman, Washington
Catalogs/Checklists: Samuel, no. 270; ACMW-FW, 1904; Reps, *Cities on Stone*, p 95; Spendlove, *Face of Early Canada*, p 77; Reps, VVUA, 3270

48. **Oregon City, Oregon**
Date: circa 1857
Title: Oregon City, Oregon
Size:
Artist: Kuchel & Dresel
Lithographer: Kuchel & Dresel
Printer: Britton & Rey [San Francisco]
Publisher:
Key/Vignettes/Misc:
Locations: Unknown
Catalogs/Checklists: Peters, COS, p. 144; Reps, VVUA, 3271

49. **Oregon City, Oregon**
Date: 1858
Title: Oregon City, Clackamas County, Oregon. 1858
Size: 15 15/16 × 25 1/16 inches (40.5 × 65.2 cm.)
Artist: Kuchel & Dresel
Lithographer:
Printer: Kuchel & Dresel, Lithographers, 176 Clay St. S. E.
Publisher: Charman & Warner, Oregon City
Key/Vignettes/Misc: 26 vignettes

Locations: ACMW-FW, UCBL-B; LC-M (facsimile)
Catalogs/Checklists: ACMW-FW, 1264; Reps, *Cities on Stone*, p. 95; LC-M, 719.1; Reps, VVUA, 3272

50. **Pendleton, Oregon**
Date: 1884
Title: Panoramic View of Pendleton, Or. County Seat of Umatilla County. 1884
Size: 13 × 21 15/16 inches (33.1 × 55.9 cm.)
Artist: H. Wellge
Lithographer:
Printer: Beck & Pauli, Milwauki, Wis.
Publisher: J. J. Stoner, Madison, Wis.
Key/Vignettes/Misc: References 2-13; 2 vignettes; unnumbered business directory
Locations: ACMW-FW; LC-M; OHS-P; LC-P
Catalogs/Checklists: ACMW-FW, 1928; Reps, *Cities on Stone*, p. 95; LC-M, 720; Reps, VVUA, 3273

51. **Pendleton, Oregon**
Date: [1888]
Title: Bird's Eye View of Pendleton, Umatilla County, Ore.
Size: 19 3/16 × 27 1/2 inches (48.8 × 70 cm.)
Artist:
Lithographer:
Printer: Dakin Publishing Co., S. F.
Publisher: East Oregonian Publishing Co., Pendleton, Or.
Key/Vignettes/Misc: References 1-33
Locations: LC-M; OHS-P
Catalogs/Checklists: LC-M, 721; Reps, VVUA, 3274

52. **Portland, Oregon**
Date: 1855
Title: Portland, Multnomah County, Oregon. 1855
Size: ["large"]
Artist: Kuchel & Dresel
Lithographer: Kuchel & Dresel
Printer: Britton & Rey [San Francisco]
Publisher:
Key/Vignettes/Misc: 40 vignettes
Locations: Unknown
Catalogs/Checklists: Peters, COS, p. 145; Reps, VVUA, 3275

53. **Portland, Oregon**
Date: 1858
Title: Portland, Multnomah County, Oregon. 1858
Size: 21 1/4 × 34 3/8 inches (54.1 × 87.5 cm.)
Artist: Kuchel & Dresel
Lithographer:
Printer: Kuchel & Dresel, Lithographers, 176 Clay St. San Francisco, Cal.
Publisher: S. J. McCormick, Franklin Book Store
Key/Vignettes/Misc: 40 vignettes
Locations: ACMW-FW; MM-NN; UCBL-B (lacks publisher's imprint); OHS-P; LC-M (facsimile)
Catalogs/Checklists: ACMW-FW, 1266; MM-NN, LP 491; LC-M, 721.1; Reps, VVUA, 3276

54. **Portland, Oregon**
   Date: circa 1861
   Title: City of Portland, Oregon
   Size: 19 1/16 × 29 1/2 inches (48.4 × 74.9 cm.)
   Artist: Grafton T. Brown
   Lithographer: C. C. Kuchel
   Printer: Britton & Co. [San Francisco]
   Publisher:
   Key/Vignettes/Misc: 22 vignettes
   Locations: ACMW-FW
   Catalogs/Checklists: Reps, *Cities on Stone*, p. 96; Reps, VVUA, 3277

55. **Portland, Oregon**
   Date: 1870
   Title: Bird's Eye View of the City of Portland, Oregon
   Size: 27 15/16 × 37 5/8 inches (71.1 × 95.7 cm.)
   Artist: C. B. Talbot
   Lithographer:
   Printer: G. T. Brown & Co. Lith. 540 Clay St. S. F.
   Publisher: P. F. Castleman
   Key/Vignettes/Misc: References 1-26, A-E
   Locations: OHS-P
   Catalogs/Checklists: Reps, *Cities on Stone*, p. 96; Reps, VVUA, 3278

56. **Portland, Oregon**
   Date: 1879 (State I)
   Title: Portland, Oregon. Population 23,000. Looking East to the Cascade
      Mountains. Price $10.
   Size: 24 × 40 3/8 inches (61.1 × 102.6 cm.)
   Artist: E. S. Glover
   Lithographer:
   Printer: A. L. Bancroft & Co., Lithographers, San Francisco, Cal.
   Publisher: E. S. Glover
   Key/Vignettes/Misc: References 1-16, 6 unnumbered references below places
      identified; unnumbered church directory
   Locations: UCBL-B; LC-M; OHS-P; LC-P
   Catalogs/Checklists: Reps, VVUA, 3279

57. **Portland, Oregon**
   Date: 1879 (State II)
   Title: Portland, Oregon. Showing Also. East Portland and the Cascade
      Mountains
   Size: 25 × 40 1/2 inches (63.6 × 103 cm.)
   Artist: E. S. Glover
   Lithographer:
   Printer: A. L. Bancroft & Co., San Francisco
   Publisher: J. K. Gill & Co., Portland
   Key/Vignettes/Misc: References 1-27; unnumbered church directory
   Locations: LC-M; UCBL-B; OHS-P
   Catalogs/Checklists: LC-M, 722; Reps, VVUA, 3280

58. **Portland, Oregon**
   Date: 1881 (State III)
   Title: Portland, Oregon. Showing Also, East Portland and the Cascade
      Mountains. Price $10
   Size: 25 × 40 3/8 inches (63.7 × 102.6 cm.)

   Artist:
   Lithographer:
   Printer: A. L. Bancroft & Co., San Francisco
   Publisher: J. K. Gill & Co., Portland
   Key/Vignettes/Misc: References 1-27; unnumbered church directory
   Locations: LC-M; CHS-C; OHS-P
   Catalogs/Checklists: LC-M, 723; Reps, VVUA, 3281

59. **Portland, Oregon**
   Date: 1888
   Title: Portland, Oregon, the Metropolis of the Pacific Northwest, as Seen
      from the Northwestern Residence Portion.
   Size: 10 × 30 1/4 inches (25.4 × 76.9 cm.)
   Artist: C. L. Smith
   Lithographer:
   Printer: West Shore Litho & Eng. Co., Portland
   Publisher: The *West Shore*, Portland, Oregon
   Key/Vignettes/Misc:
   Locations: OUL-E; HEHL; ACMW-FW; LC-P
   Catalogs/Checklists: Reps, VVUA, 3282

60. **Portland, Oregon**
   Date: 1889
   Title: Portland, Oregon, and its Surroundings, 1889
   Size: 12 5/8 × 19 1/8 inches (32.2 × 48.7 cm.)
   Artist:
   Lithographer:
   Printer: Lewis & Dryden Print Co. Lith. Portland Or.
   Publisher: Oregon Immigration Board
   Key/Vignettes/Misc:
   Locations: OHS-P
   Catalogs/Checklists: Reps, VVUA, 3283

61. **Portland, Oregon**
   Date: 1890
   Title: Portland, Oregon 1890.
   Size: 30 1/8 × 44 7/16 inches (76.7 × 113 cm.)
   Artist: B. W. Pierce
   Lithographer:
   Printer: Elliott Publishing Co., San Francisco
   Publisher: Clohessy & Strengle, Portland
   Key/Vignettes/Misc: References 1-130; 29 vignettes
   Locations: OHS-P; LC-M; UCBL-B; WHPL-D
   Catalogs/Checklists: LC-M, 724; Reps, *Cities on Stone*, p. 96; Reps, VVUA, 3284

62. **Portland, Oregon**
   Date: 1890
   Title: Portland, Oregon; and Surroundings. 1890. Looking North
   Size: 18 1/4 × 24 7/8 inches (46.4 × 63.4 cm.)
   Artist:
   Lithographer:
   Printer: Elliott Pub. Co. 120 Sutter St. S. F.
   Publisher:
   Key/Vignettes/Misc:
   Locations: OHS-P
   Catalogs/Checklists: Reps, VVUA, 3285

63. **Portland, Oregon**
Date: circa 1890
Title: Portland's Willamette-Columbia Peninsula, Portland, Or.
Size: 22 1/8 × 34 3/4 inches (56.3 × 88.4 cm.)
Artist: Elliott Pub. Co.
Lithographer:
Printer: Elliott Pub. Co. 120 Sutter St. S. F. Cal.
Publisher:
Key/Vignettes/Misc: References 1-2; 1 vignette
Locations: OHS-P
Catalogs/Checklists: Reps, VVUA, 3286

64. **Portland, Oregon**
Date: 1893
Title: Portland, Or. Population 80,000
Size: 34 3/4 × 47 3/4 inches (88.3 × 121.5 cm.)
Artist:
Lithographer:
Printer: The Lewis & Dryden Lithographing Co., Portland, Oregon
Publisher: The Oregon Immigration Board
Key/Vignettes/Misc: 5 unnumbered references above places identified; 31 vignettes; description
Locations: OHS-P
Catalogs/Checklists: Reps, VVUA, 3287

65. **Portland, Oregon**
Date: 1904
Title: Bird's-Eye View of Portland, Oregon, "The Rose City." Looking in North-Easterly Direction, Showing 4 1/2 Miles of Willamette River.
Size: 38 1/4 × 56 1/2 inches (97.3 × 143.7 cm.)
Artist:
Lithographer:
Printer: Mutual Label & Lith Co., Portland, Or.
Publisher: Lawrence Publishing Co. (copyright)
Key/Vignettes/Misc: 27 vignettes; 2 portraits
Locations: OHS-P
Catalogs/Checklists: Reps, VVUA, 3288

66. **Portland, Oregon**
Date: 1909
Title: [Untitled View of Portland, Oregon, Vancouver, Washington and the Willamette Valley]
Size: 17 7/16 × 47 13/16 inches (44.4 × 121.7 cm.)
Artist: Gibson Catlett
Lithographer:
Printer: The James Printing Co.
Publisher: A. E. Chisholm, 212 Henry Building, Portland, Oregon
Key/Vignettes/Misc:
Locations: OHS-P
Catalogs/Checklists: Reps, VVUA, 3289

67. **Roseburg, Oregon**
Date: [1888]
Title: Roseburg, Oregon
Size: 13 7/8 × 19 inches (35.3 × 48.4 cm.)
Artist:

Lithographer:
Printer:
Publisher: The *West Shore* [Portland]
Key/Vignettes/Misc:
Locations: OHS-P
Catalogs/Checklists: Reps, VVUA, 3290

68. **Roseburg, Oregon**
Date: [1890-91]
Title: Birds Eye View of Roseburg, Douglas County, Oregon—Compliments of the Hendricks Review Real Estate Company, Roseburg, Oregon
Size: 14 × 18 inches (35.6 × 45.9 cm.)
Artist:
Lithographer:
Printer:
Publisher: W. W. Elliott, Pub. Co. 120 Sutter St., S. F.
Key/Vignettes/Misc: 12 vignettes
Locations: Douglas County Museum, Roseburg, Oregon
Catalogs/Checklists: Reps, VVUA, 3291

69. **Salem, Oregon**
Date: 1858
Title: Salem, Marion County, Oregon. 1858.
Size: 15 13/16 × 25 5/8 inches (40.2 × 65.1 cm.)
Artist: Kuchel & Dresel
Lithographer:
Printer: Kuchel & Dresel, San Francisco
Publisher: W. C. Griswold & Co., Salem
Key/Vignettes/Misc: 26 vignettes
Locations: ACMW-FW; CHS-C; LC-M (facsimile)
Catalogs/Checklists: ACMW-FW, 1268; Peters, COS, p. 145; LC-M, 724.1; Reps, VVUA, 3292

70. **Salem, Oregon**
Date: 1876
Title: Bird's Eye View of Salem, Oregon From the West Looking East. 1876
Size: 20 3/4 × 29 9/16 inches (52.8 × 75.2 cm.)
Artist: E. S. Glover, from photograph by F. A. Smith
Lithographer:
Printer: A. L. Bancroft & Co., Lithographers, San Francisco, California
Publisher: F. A. Smith, Salem, Oregon
Key/Vignettes/Misc: References A-C, E, F, H, I; unnumbered directory
Locations: LC-M; UCBL-B
Catalogs/Checklists: LC-M, 525; Reps, *Cities on Stone*, p. 96; Reps, VVUA, 3293

71. **Salem, Oregon**
Date: 1890 (State I)
Title: The City of Salem, Capital of Oregon
Size: 23 7/8 × 32 11/16 inches (60.8 × 83.2 cm.)
Artist: E. S. Moore
Lithographer:
Printer:
Publisher: [no publisher]
Key/Vignettes/Misc: References 1-19; 25 vignettes
Locations: OHS-P
Catalogs/Checklists: Reps, VVUA, 3294

72. **Salem, Oregon**
Date: 1890 (State II)
Title: The City of Salem, Capital of Oregon
Size: 23 7/8 × 32 11/16 inches (60.8 × 83.2 cm.)
Artist: E. S. Moore
Lithographer:
Printer:
Publisher: Salem Board of Trade
Key/Vignettes/Misc: References 1-19; 25 vignettes
Locations: OHS-P
Catalogs/Checklists: Reps, VVUA, 3295

73. **Salem, Oregon**
Date: [1905]
Title: Capital City of Oregon, Salem
Size: 27 × 35 inches (68.6 × 89 cm.)
Artist:
Lithographer:
Printer: Mutual L. & Lith. Co., Portland
Publisher: E. Koppe & Ch. Fromm
Key/Vignettes/Misc: 2 vignettes
Locations: LC-M
Catalogs /Checklists: LC-M, 726; Reps, VVUA, 3296

74. **Stanley, Oregon**
Date: [1890]
Title: Map and Plainly Stated Facts About Stanley.
Size: 23 5/8 × 18 1/8 inches (60 × 46 cm.)
Artist:
Lithographer:
Printer: Dickman-Jones, San Francisco
Publisher: Stites, Kerr & Co., Portland
Key/Vignettes/Misc:
Locations: OUL-E
Catalogs/Checklists: Reps, VVUA, 3297

75. **The Dalles, Oregon**
Date: 1858
Title: The Dalles, Wasco County, Oregon, 1858.
Size: 13 3/4 × 20 inches (34.8 × 50.7 cm.)
Artist: Kuchel & Dresel
Printer: Kuchel & Dresel, Lithographers, 176 Clay St. S. Francisco
Publisher: W. L. Demoss
Key/Vignettes/Misc: 16 vignettes
Locations: ACMW-FW; UCBL-B; CHS-C; OHS-P (title cropped)
Catalogs/Checklists: ACMW-FW, 1256; Reps, *Cities on Stone,* p. 92; Reps, VVUA, 3298

76. **The Dalles, Oregon**
Date: 1884
Title: Panoramic View of the City of The Dalles, Or. County Seat of Wasco County 1884.
Size: 13 1/2 × 24 1/8 inches (34.4 × 61.4 cm.)
Artist: H. Wellge
Lithographer:
Printer: Beck & Pauli, Litho. Milwaukee, Wis.

Publisher: J. J. Stoner, Madison, Wis.
Key/Vignettes/Mis: References 1-17
Locations: LC-M; OHS-P
Catalogs/Checklists: LC-M, 727; Reps, VVUA, 3299

77. **The Dalles, Oregon**
Date: [no date]
Title: Panoramic View of the Dalles, Oregon
Size: 10 × 16 inches (25.4 × 40.7 cm.)
Artist:
Lithographer:
Printer: The *West Shore*, Portland, Oregon
Publisher: The *West Shore*, Portland, Oregon
Key/Vignettes/Misc:
Locations: MM-NN
Catalogs/Checklists: MM-NN, LP 860; Reps, VVUA 3300

WASHINGTON

78. **Cheney, Washington**
Date: 1884
Title: Bird's Eye View of Cheney, Wash. Ter. County Seat of Spokane County. 1884
Size: 9 7/16 X 19 15/16 inches (23.9 × 50.6 cm.)
Artist: H Wellge
Lithographer:
Printer: Beck & Pauli Lith. Milwaukee, Wis.
Publisher: J. J. Stoner, Madison, Wis.
Key/Vignettes/Misc: References 1-17; 2 vignettes; unnumbered business directory
Locations: LC-M; EWHS-S; LC-P
Catalogs/Checklists: LC-M, 967; Reps, VVUA, 4153

79. **Dayton, Washington**
Date: 1884
Title: Panoramic View of Dayton, W. T., County Seat of Columbia County. 1884.
Size: 10 5/8 × 24 3/4 inches (27 × 63 cm.)
Artist: H Wellge
Lithographer:
Printer: Beck & Pauli, Litho. Milwaukee, Wis.
Publisher:
Key/Vignettes/Misc: References 1-24; 1 vignette; unnumbered business directory
Locations: LC-M
Catalogs/Checklists: LC-M, 968; Reps, VVUA, 4154

East Olympia, Washington
Date: 1879
See **Olympia, Washington,** 1879

80. **Ellensburg, Washington**
Date: 1890
Title: Ellensburgh, Washington—Brick Buildings Erected Since the Great Fire of July 4, 1889.
Size: 23 3/6 × 35 3/8 inches (59 × 90 cm.)

Artist: Routledge
Lithographer:
Printer:
Publisher: The *West Shore*, Portland, Oregon
Key/Vignettes/Misc: 26 vignettes
Locations: OUL-E
Catalogs/Checklists: Reps, VVUA, 4155

81. **Everett, Washington**
Date: 1893
Title: Birdseyeview [sic] of Everett, Washington. 1893
Size:
Artist:
Lithographer:
Printer:
Publisher: Brown's Land and Engineering Co. Inc.
Key/Vignettes/Misc: References 1-60; 10 vignettes; description
Locations: UWL-S; Snohomish County Museum and Historical Association, Everett, Washington
Catalogs/Checklists: Reps, VVUA, 4156

82. **Fairhaven, Washington**
Date: 1891
Title: Fairhaven, Washington 1891
Size: 23 3/16 × 38 1/2 inches (59 × 98 cm.)
Artist: B. W. Pierce
Lithographer: R. H.
Printer: Elliott Pub. Co. 120 Sutter St. S. F.
Publisher: Fairhaven Land Co.
Key/Vignettes/Misc:
Locations: NHM-LA; WHS-M; LC-M (photo)
Catalogs/Checklists: LC-M, 968.1; Reps, VVUA, 4157

83. **Goldendale, Washington**
Date: No Date
Title: [Goldendale, Washington]
Size: 19 1/2 × 25 1/2 inches (49.6 × 64.9 cm.)
Artist:
Lithographer:
Printer: Lewis & Dryden . . . Portland, Or.
Publisher: Goldendale Sentinel
Key/Vignettes/Misc: 3 vignettes; advertisements
Locations: Klickitat County Historical Society, Goldendale, Washington
Catalogs/Checklists: Reps, VVUA, 4158

84. **Montesano, Washington**
Date: [1890]
Title: Bird's Eye View of Montesano, Chehalis County, W. T.
Size: 12 5/8 × 28 5/16 inches (32 × 72 cm.)
Artist: J. E. Calder
Lithographer:
Printer: Elliott Publishing Co. San Francisco
Publisher: J. E. Calder, Real Estate Dealer
Key/Vignettes/Misc:
Locations: OUL-E
Catalogs/Checklists: Reps, VVUA, 4159

New Tacoma, Washington
Date: 1878
See **Tacoma, Washington,** 1878

85. **North Yakima**
Date: 1889
Title: View of the City of North Yakima, Washington
Size: 18 1/16 × 31 inches (46 × 79 cm.)
Artist: S.[yd] W. Arnold
Lithographer:
Printer:
Publisher: Spike & Arnold Map Publishing Co.
Key/Vignettes/Misc: References 1-51; 11-61, and 41 unnumbered residences; 2 vignettes
Locations: LC-M; WSHS-T; Yakima Valley Museum and Historial Association, Yakima, Washington
Catalogs/Checklists: LC-M, 969; Reps, VVUA, 4160

86. **Olympia, Washington**
Date: 1879
Title: Bird's-Eye View of the City of Olympia, East Olympia and Tumwater, Puget Sound, Washington Territory.
Size: 18 7/8 × 29 7/8 inches (48.1 × 76 cm.)
Artist: E. S. Glover
Lithographer:
Printer: A. L. Bancroft & Co., Lithographers, San Francisco
Publisher: E. S. Glover (copyright)
Key/Vignettes/Misc: References 1-15; 2 unnumbered references below places identified
Locations: ACMW-FW; LC-M; UCBL-B; BPL-R; UWL-S; WSHS-T; EWHS-S; LC-P
Catalogs/Checklists: LC-M, 970; Reps, *Cities on Stone,* p. 95; Reps, VVUA, 4161

87. **Olympia, Washington**
Date: 1903
Title: Olympia the Capital on Puget Sound, Washington the City of Refinement and Cultivation, Manufacture and Commerce, Educational Facilities, etc.
Size: 17 1/2 × 20 1/2 inches (44.5 × 52.2 cm.)
Artist: Edw. Lange
Lithographer:
Printer: Franklin Engraving & Electrotyping Co., Chicago
Publisher: Edw. Lange, Olympia, Wash.
Key/Vignettes/Misc: 17 vignettes
Locations: LC-M
Catalogs/Checklists: LC-M, 971; Reps, VVUA, 4162

88. **Port Gamble, Washington**
Date: [1862-64] (State I)
Title: Puget Mill Co.'s Mills, Teekalet W. T. M. C. Talbot & Co. San Francisco, California
Size:
Artist: T.[rautman] Grob
Lithographer: T. Grob
Printer: Nagel, Fishbourne & Kuchel, 529 Clay St., San Francisco, Ca.
Publisher:

Key/Vignettes/Misc:
Locations: UWL-S (photo)
Catalogs/Checklists: Reps, VVUA, 4163

89. **Port Gamble, Washington**
Date: [1862-64] (State II)
Title: Puget Mill Co.'s Mills. Teekalet, W. T. Pope and Talbot, San Fran-
cisco, California
Size:
Artist: T.[rautman] Grob
Lithographer: T. Grob
Printer: Nagel, Fishbourne & Kuchel, 529 Clay Street, San Francisco, Ca.
Publisher:
Key/Vignettes/Misc:
Locations: UWL-S (photo)
Catalogs/Checklists: Peters, COS, p. 172; Reps, VVUA, 4164

90. **Port Ludlow, Washington**
Date: circa 1862
Title: Port Ludlow, Puget Sound, W. T. Amos Phinney & Co.'s Mills.
Size: 18 1/4 × 24 5/8 inches (46.4 x 62.7 cm.)
Artist: C. B. Gifford
Lithographer: C. B. Gifford
Printer: T. Nagel
Publisher:
Key/Vignettes/Misc:
Locations: UWL-S
Catalogs/Checklists: Reps, VVUA, 4165

91. **Port Townsend, Washington**
Date: 1878
Title: Bird's Eye View of Port Townsend, Puget Sound, Washington Ter-
ritory. From North-East. 1878
Size: 15 7/8 × 24 7/16 inches (40.4 × 62.2 cm.)
Artist: E. S. Glover
Lithographer:
Printer: A. L. Bancroft & Co. Lith., San Francisco, Cal.
Publisher: E. S. Glover, Portland, Oregon
Key/Vignettes/Misc: References A-T
Locations: LC-M; BPL-R; MM-NN; UCBL-B; LC-P
Catalogs/Checklists: LC-M, 972; MM-NN, LP 195; Reps, VVUA, 4166

92. **Port Townsend, Washington**
Date: [before 1889]
Title: Port Townsend, W. T.
Size: 19 1/8 × 25 3/4 inches (48.7 × 65.6 cm.)
Artist:
Lithographer:
Printer:
Publisher: Townsend *Call*
Key/Vignettes/Misc: 4 views surrounded by advertisement
Locations: SHS-S
Catalogs/Checklists: Reps, VVUA, 4167

93. **Roslyn, Washington**
Date: [189-?]
Title: A General View of Roslyn Looking Toward Clealum.

Size:
Artist: Edw. Lange
Lithographer:
Printer:
Publisher: Northern Pacific Coal Co.
Key/Vignettes/Misc: References 1-20; 8 vignettes
Locations: SHS-S (photo)
Catalogs/Checklists: Reps, VVUA, 4168

94. **Seattle, Washington**
Date: 1878
Title: Bird's-Eye View of the City of Seattle, Puget Sound, Washington Ter-
ritory, 1878.
Size: 19 1/2 × 30 1/2 inches (49.5 × 77.4 cm.)
Artist: E. S. Glover
Lithographer:
Printer: A. L. Bancroft & Co., Lithographers, San Francisco
Publisher: E. S. Glover (copyright)
Key/Vignettes/Misc: References 1-20, A-B
Locations: ACMW-FW; LC-M; UCBL-B; LC-P
Catalogs/Checklists: LC-M, 973; Reps, *Cities on Stone*, p. 98; Reps, VVUA, 4169

95. **Seattle, Washington**
Date: circa 1879
Title: Seattle, Washington Territory
Size: 10 × 16 3/16 inches (25.5 × 41.2 cm.)
Artist:
Lithographer:
Printer: The *West Shore,* Portland Oregon
Publisher:
Key/Vignettes/Misc: 1 vignette
Locations: NYP-S
Catalogs/Checklists: Reps, VVUA, 4170

96. **Seattle, Washington**
Date: 1884
Title: Bird's Eye View of the City of Seattle, WT. Puget Sound. County Seat
of King County. 1884.
Size: 16 1/4 × 32 5/8 inches (41.4 × 82.8 cm.)
Artist: H. Wellge
Lithographer:
Printer: Beck & Pauli, Litho. Milwaukee, Wis.
Publisher: J. J. Stoner, Madison, Wis.
Key/Vignettes/Misc: References 2-10; 12-37; A-H, J-M; 2 vignettes
Locations: CHS-C; NYP-S; SHS-S; UWL-S; Seattle Public Library, Seattle,
Washington; NYH-NY; LC-M
Catalogs/Checklists: Stokes 1884—G-86; Reps, *Cities on Stone*, p. 98; LC-M,
974; Reps, VVUA, 4171

97. **Seattle, Washington**
Date: 1884
Title: Seattle, W. T. 1884
Size: 8 1/2 × 27 1/2 inches (21.6 × 69.9 cm.)
Artist: A. Burr
Lithographer: C. L. Smith
Printer:

Publisher: The *West Shore*, Portland, Oregon
Key/Vignettes/Misc:
Locations: ACMW-FW; UWL-S; SHS-S
Catalogs/Checklists: ACMW-FW, 942; Reps, VVUA, 4172

98. **Seattle, Washington**
Date: 1889
Title: Seattle, 1889
Size: 25 15/16 × 37 15/16 inches (63.5 × 96.5 cm.) (facsimile)
Artist:
Lithographer:
Printer:
Publisher: Llewellyn, Dodge & Co., Seattle
Key/Vignettes/Misc: References 1-58; 20 vignettes
Locations: SHS-S (facsimile); UCBL-B
Catalogs/Checklists: Reps, VVUA, 4173

99. **Seattle, Washington**
Date: 1889
Title: Seattle, 1889
Size: 22 1/4 × 35 3/4 inches (56.6 × 90.9 cm.)
Artist: C. L.(?) Stubbs
Lithographer:
Printer: Schmidt L. & L. Co., San Francisco
Publisher: The Elliott Pub. Co., 120 Sutter St. San Francisco
Key/Vignettes/Misc: References 1-58; 20 vignettes
Locations: UCBL-B; SHS-S
Catalogs/Checklists: Reps, VVUA, 4174

100. **Seattle, Washington**
Date: 1891
Title: Birds Eye View of Seattle and Environs. Kings County, Wash., 1891 Eighteen Months After the Great Fire.
Size: 33 1/4 × 50 1/16 inches (84.6 × 127.3 cm.)
Artist: Augustus Koch
Lithographer:
Printer: Hughes Litho Co. Chicago
Publisher: Augustus Koch (copyright)
Key/Vignettes/Misc: References 1-120; A-I, K-L
Locations: LC-M; ACMW-FW; UCBL-B; UWL-S; Seattle Public Library, Seattle, Washington; LC-P
Catalogs/Checklists: LC-M, 975; Reps, *Cities on Stone*, p. 98; Reps, VVUA, 4175

101. **Seattle, Washington**
Date: circa 1903
Title: Main Business District Periscopic Seattle.
Size: 19 1/4 × 20 13/16 inches (49 × 53 cm.)
Artist: Ross W. Tulloch
Lithographer:
Printer:
Publisher: Periscopic Map Co., Seattle
Key/Vignettes/Misc:
Locations: LC-M
Catalogs/Checklists: LC-M, 976; Reps, VVUA, 4176

102. **Seattle, Washington**
Date: 1904
Title: Bird's Eye View City of Seattle
Size: 25 3/4 × 41 3/8 inches (65.5 × 105.3)
Artist:
Lithographer: FL
Printer: Tucker Hanford Co. Seattle
Publisher: Seattle . . . [missing or illegible]
Key/Vignettes/Misc:
Locations: UWL-S
Catalogs/Checklists: Reps, VVUA, 4177

103. **Seattle, Washington**
Date: circa 1925
Title: Seattle Birdseye View of Portion of City and Vicinity.
Size: 30 5/8 × 55 inches (78 × 140 cm.)
Artist: Edwin C. Poland
Lithographer:
Printer:
Publisher: Kroll Map Company, Seattle
Key/Vignettes/Misc:
Locations: LC-M (photo)
Catalogs/Checklists: LC-M, 977; Reps, VVUA, 4178

104. **Seattle, Washington**
Date: No Date
Title: Bird's Eye View of the Waterfront, Seattle, W. T.
Size: 9 3/8 × 15 7/8 inches (23.8 × 40.4 cm.)
Artist:
Lithographer: A. G. Walling
Printer:
Publisher: The *West Shore*, Portland, Oregon
Key/Vignettes/Misc:
Locations: MM-NN
Catalogs/Checklists: MM-NN, LP 859; Reps, VVUA, 4179

105. **Snohomish, Washington**
Date: No Date
Title: Bird-Eye View of Snohomish, Washington
Size: 9 7/8 × 16 1/8 inches (25.1 × 41 cm.)
Artist:
Lithographer:
Printer: North Pacific History Company, Portland, Oregon
Publisher:
Key/Vignettes/Misc: 3 vignettes
Locations: Snohomish Public Library, Snohomish, Washington.
Catalogs/Checklists: Reps, VVUA, 4180

106. **Spokane, Washington**
Date: 1884
Title: Bird's Eye View of Spokane Falls, W. T., 1884
Size: 16 3/4 × 26 3/4 inches (42.5 × 67.8 cm.)
Artist: H. Wellge
Lithographer:
Printer: Beck & Pauli, Milwaukee
Publisher: J. J. Stoner, Madison

Key/Vignettes/Misc: References 1-30; 4 vignettes; unnumbered business
directory
Locations: Washington State University Libraries, Pullman, Washington;
EWHS-S
Catalogs/Checklists: Reps, VVUA, 4181

107. **Spokane, Washington**
Date: circa 1885
Title: Spokane Falls, W. T. and Surroundings
Size: 12 5/16 × 19 3/4 inches (31.4 × 50.3 cm.)
Artist: W. D. Andrew
Lithographer:
Printer: Waugaman-Lith-532 Commercial St. S. F.
Publisher: *The Wasp*
Key/Vignettes/Misc: 7 vignettes
Locations: UCBL-B
Catalogs/Checklists: Reps, VVUA, 4182

108. **Spokane, Washington**
Date: [1888]
Title: Spokane Falls, W. T.
Size: 16 7/8 (cropped) × 20 3/8 inches (42.9 × 51.9 cm.)
Artist: J. T. Pickett
Lithographer:
Printer: Lewis & Dryden Print Co. Lith.
Publisher:
Key/Vignettes/Misc: 10 vignettes
Locations: OHS-P
Catalogs/Checklists: Reps, VVUA, 4183

109. **Spokane, Washington**
Date: [Before 1890]
Title: Spokane Falls and Her Natural Resources, the Variety and Extent of
which are Not Equalled in Any City in the World
Size: 5 3/4 × 12 3/4 inches (14.7 × 32.5 cm.)
Artist:
Lithographer:
Printer: Gies & Co., Buffalo, N.Y.
Publisher:
Key/Vignettes/Misc:
Locations: UCBL-B
Catalogs/Checklists: LC-M, 978.1; Reps, VVUA, 4184

110. **Spokane, Washington**
Date: 1905
Title: Spokane, Washington
Size: 39 × 60 inches (99.2 × 152.6 cm.)
Artist:
Lithographer:
Printer:
Publisher: John W. Graham & Co., Spokane, Wash.
Key/Vignettes/Misc: 1 vignette
Locations: LC-M
Catalogs/Checklists: LC-M, 978; Reps, VVUA, 4185

111. **Steilacoom, Washington**
Date: 1862
Title: View of Steilacoom, W. T.
Size: 17 1/2 × 26 inches (44.5 × 66.2 cm.)
Artist: T. [rautman] Grob
Lithographer:
Printer: L. Nagel
Publisher:
Key/Vignettes/Misc:
Locations: CHS-C
Catalogs/Checklists: Reps, VVUA, 4186

112. **Tacoma, Washington**
Date: 1878
Title: View of New Tacoma and Mount Rainier, Puget Sound, Washington
Territory. Terminus of the Northern Pacific Railroad.
Size: 16 1/8 × 24 1/8 inches (41 X 61.4 cm.)
Artist: E. S. Glover
Lithographer:
Printer: A. L. Bancroft & Co. Litho., San Francisco, Cal.
Publisher: E. S. Glover, Portland Oregon
Key/Vignettes/Misc:
Locations: NYP-S; LC-M; UCBL-B; WSHS-T
Catalogs/Checklists: Stokes P. 1877—G-92; Peters, COS, pp. 55, 124; LC-M,
979; Reps, *Cities on Stone*, p. 98; Reps, VVUA, 4187

113. **Tacoma, Washington**
Date: 1884
Title: View of the City of Tacoma, W. T. Puget-Sound County Seat of
Pierce Cty Pacific Terminus of the N. P. R. R. 1884.
Size: 14 5/8 × 32 3/8 inches (37.2 × 82.4 cm)
Artist: H. Wellge
Lithographer:
Printer: Beck & Pauli, Litho. Milwaukee, Wis.
Publisher: J. J. Stoner, Madison, Wis.
Key/Vignettes/Misc: References 1-31; 1 vignette
Locations: ACMW-FW; LC-M; NYP-S; WSHS-T; EWHS-S; Tacoma Public
Library
Catalogs/Checklists: ACMW-FW, 1930; LC-M, 980; Reps, *Cities on Stone*, p.
98; Reps, VVUA, 4188

114. **Tacoma, Washington**
Date: 1885
Title: City of Tacoma, W. T. Western Terminus of N. P. R. R. Puget Sound.
1885.
Size: 15 3/4 × 33 1/4 inches (40.1 × 84.6 cm.)
Artist:
Lithographer:
Printer:
Publisher:
Key/Vignettes/Misc: References 1-35
Locations: LC-M; Tacoma Public Library (cropped)
Catalogs/Checklists: LC-M, 981; Reps, VVUA, 4189

115. **Tacoma, Washington**
Date: 1889
Title: Tacoma 1889.
Size:
Artist:
Lithographer:
Printer: Elliott Pub Co., 120 Sutter St. S. F.
Publisher: Geo. W. Traver
Key/Vignettes/Misc: References 1-88; 19 vignettes
Locations: Tacoma Public Library (facsimile)
Catalogs/Checklists: Reps, VVUA, 4190

116. **Tacoma, Washington**
Date: 1889
Title: The City of Tacoma
Size: 18 × 36 inches (45.8 × 91.5 cm.)
Artist:
Lithographer:
Printer: Lewis & Dryden Printing Co.
Publisher: J. B. Gromwell Co. (Real Estate)
Key/Vignettes/Misc:
Locations: MM-NN
Catalogs/Checklists: MM-NN, LP, 4851; Reps, VVUA, 4191

117. **Tacoma, Washington**
Date: 1890
Title: Tacoma
Size: 21 7/8 × 35 13/16 inches (55.7 × 91.1 cm.)
Artist:
Lithographer:
Printer: Elliott Litho Co., S. F.
Publisher: Geo. W. Traver [Tacoma]
Key/Vignettes/Misc: References 1-99, A-G; 16 vignettes
Locations: LC-M (photo); WSHS-T; CHS-C; PAC
Catalogs/Checklists: LC-M, 982.1; Reps, VVUA, 4192

118. **Tacoma, Washington**
Date: 1890
Title: Tacoma. Western Terminus of the Northern Pacific Railroad.
Size: 32 × 43 1/2 inches (81.4 × 110.7 cm.)
Artist: Will Carson
Lithographer:
Printer:
Publisher: Will Carson (copyright)
Key/Vignettes/Misc: References 1-45; 11 vignettes
Locations: LC-M; UCBL-B; WSHS-T
Catalogs/Checklists: LC-M, 982; Reps, VVUA, 4193

119. **Tacoma, Washington**
Date: 1893
Title: Tacoma, Washington. 1893
Size: 26 1/4 × 41 1/8 inches (66.8 × 105 cm.)
Artist:
Lithographer:
Printer: The Blachly Co. Lith. Tacoma
Publisher: J. R. McIntyre, Tacoma

Key/Vignettes/Misc: References 1-60; 20 vignettes
Locations: WSHS-T
Catalogs/Checklists: Reps, VVUA, 4194

Teekalet, Washington
[1862-1864]
See **Port Gamble, Washington** [1862-1864].

Tumwater, Washington
Date: 1879
See **Olympia, Washington**, 1879.

120. **Utsalady, Washington**
Date: 1862
Title: Grennan & Cranney's Saw Mills, Utsalady, Camano Island, Puget Sound, W. T. 1862.
Size: 14 1/2 × 23 3/4 inches (36.9 × 60.5 cm.)
Artist:
Lithographer: C. B. Gifford
Printer: I. Nagel, S. F.
Publisher:
Key/Vignettes/Misc: Description
Locations: UWL-S
Catalogs/Checklists: Reps, VVUA, 4195

121. **Vancouver, Washington**
Date: 1858
Title: Vancouver, Clark County, W. T. 1858.
Size: 13 7/8 × 20 1/8 inches (35.1 × 51 cm.)
Artist: Kuchel & Dresel
Lithographer: Kuchel & Dresel
Printer: Kuchel & Dresel, Lithographers, 176 Clay St. S. Francisco, Cal.
Publisher: Camp & Co., Vancouver
Key/Vignettes/Misc: 19 vignettes
Locations: ACMW-FW
Catalogs/Checklists: ACMW-FW, 1276; Reps, VVUA, 4196

122. **Vancouver, Washington**
Date: circa 1858
Title: Vancouver, Washington Territory
Size: ["medium"]
Artist: Kuchel & Dresel
Lithographer: Kuchel & Dresel
Printer: Britton & Rey
Publisher:
Key/Vignettes/Misc:
Locations: Unknown
Catalogs/Checklists: Peters, COS, p. 145; Reps, VVUA, 4197

123. **Waitsburg, Washington**
Date: 1884
Title: Panoramic View of Waitsburg, W. T. Walla-Walla County. 1884.
Size: 13 × 19 inches (33.1 × 48.3 cm.)
Artist:
Lithographer:
Printer: Beck & Pauli, Litho. Milwaukee, Wis.

Publisher: Ruger & Stoner, Madison, Wis.
Key/Vignettes/Misc: References 1-23; 1 vignette
Locations: Waitsburg Historical Society, Waitsburg, Washington
Catalogs/Checklists: Reps, VVUA, 4198

124. **Walla Walla, Washington**
Date: 1866
Title: [Walla Walla, Washington] 1866
Size: 18 3/8 × 26 7/8 inches (46.8 × 68.4 cm.)
Artist: From photographs by P. F. Castleman
Lithographer:
Printer: Grafton T. Brown & Co., Lith. 543 Clay St. S. F. Cal.
Publisher:
Key/Vignettes/Misc: 29 vignettes
Locations: PLW-WW
Catalogs/Checklists: Reps, VVUA, 4199

125. **Walla Walla, Washington**
Date: 1876
Title: Bird's Eye View of Walla Walla, Washington Territory, 1876
Size: 19 × 28 1/2 inches (48.2 × 71.1 cm.)
Artist: E. S. Glover
Lithographer:
Printer: A. L. Bancroft & Co., Lithographers, San Francisco, Cal.
Publisher: Everts & Able, Walla Walla
Key/Vignettes/Misc: References 1-22
Locations: LC-M
Catalogs/Checklists: LC-M, 983; Reps, *Cities on Stone*, p. 99; Reps, VVUA, 4200

126. **Walla Walla, Washington**
Date: 1881
Title: [Untitled]
Size: 10 1/2 × 16 3/4 inches (26.7 × 42.7 cm.)
Artist: A. Burr
Lithographer:
Printer: A. G. Walling, Portland, Oregon
Publisher: [F. F. Adams, Walla Walla, Washington]
Key/Vignettes/Misc: Advertisement
Locations: PLW-WW
Catalogs/Checklists: Reps, VVUA, 4201

127. **Walla Walla, Washington**
Date: 1884
Title: Panoramic View of the City of Walla-Walla, W. T. County Seat of Walla Walla Co. 1884
Size: 18 × 27 1/2 inches (45.9 × 69.9 cm.)
Artist: H Wellge
Lithographer:
Printer: Beck & Pauli, Milwaukee, Wisconsin
Publisher: J. J. Stoner, Madison, Wisconsin
Key/Vignettes/Misc: References A-H, 2-21; unnumbered business directory
Locations: LC-M; PLW-WW
Catalogs/Checklists: LC-M, 984; Reps, VVUA, 4202

128. **Walla Walla, Washington**
Date: 1890

Title: Walla Walla Washington (1889)
Size: 22 3/8 × 35 3/4 inches (57 × 90.9 cm.)
Artist: B. W. Pierce
Lithographer:
Printer: Elliott Litho & Pub. Co. S. F.
Publisher: Elliott Litho & Pub. Co. S. F.
Key/Vignettes/Misc: References 1-44; 28 vignettes; advertisement
Locations: PLW-WW
Catalogs/Checklists: Reps, VVUA, 4203

129. **Walla Walla, Washington**
Date: 1890
Title: Walla Walla Washington The Garden City 1889
Size: 22 3/8 × 35 3/4 inches (57 × 90.9 cm.)
Artist: B. W. Pierce
Lithographer:
Printer: Elliott Litho & Pub. Co. S. F.
Publisher: Elliott Litho & Pub. Co. S. F.
Key/Vignettes/Misc: References 1-44; 27 vignettes
Locations: PLW-WW
Catalogs/Checklists: Reps, VVUA, 4204

130. **Yakima, Washington**
Date: 1935
Title: Early Days in Yakima, Washington Territory, Settled 1885
Size: 14 × 19 3/16 inches (35.7 × 48.8 cm.)
Artist: H. D. Guie & C. A. Badeau
Lithographer:
Printer: Republic Publishing Co., Yakima, Washington
Publisher: Republic Publishing Co., Yakima, Washington
Key/Vignettes/Misc:
Locations: Yakima Valley Museum & Historical Association, Yakima, Washington
Catalogs/Checklists: Reps, VVUA, 4205

Catalogs and Checklists

ACMW-FW Amon Carter Museum of Western Art. *Catalog of the Collection, 1972.* Fort Worth: Amon Carter Museum of Western Art, 1973.

LC-M U. S. Library of Congress, *Panoramic Maps of Cities in the United States and Canada: A Checklist of Maps in the Collections of the Library of Congress, Geography and Map Division.* John R. Hébert and Patrick E. Dempsey, comps. Washington D.C.: Library of Congress, 1984.

MM-NN Mariners Museum. *Catalog of Marine Prints and Paintings, Mariners Museum Library, Newport News, Virginia.* 3 volumes. Boston: G. K. Hall & Co., 1964.

PAC (1976) Public Archives of Canada. "Bird's-Eye Views of Canadian Cities: An Exhibition of Panoramic Maps (1865-1905) . . . Exhibition handlist reproduced from typewritten copy. Ottawa: Public Archives of Canada, 1976.

PAC Public Archives of Canada. National Map Collection, *Catalogue of the National Map Collection, Public Archives of Canada.* 15 volumes. Boston: G. K. Hall, 1976.

Peters COS Peters, Harry T. *California on Stone.* Garden City, New York: Doubleday, Doran & Company, Inc., 1935.

Reps, *Cities on Stone*

Reps, John W. *Cities on Stone: Nineteenth Century Lithographic Images of the Urban West.* Fort Worth, Texas: Amon Carter Museum of Western Art, 1976.

Reps, VVUA Reps, John W. *Views and Viewmakers of Urban America: Lithographs of Cities in the United States and Canada With Notes on the Artists and Publishers and a Union Catalog of Their Work, 1825-1925.* Columbia, Missouri: University of Missouri Press, 1984.

Robertson Toronto Public Libraries. *Landmarks of Canada: A Guide to the J. Ross Robertson Canadian Historical Collection in the Toronto Public Library.* 3 volumes. Toronto: Toronto Public Library, 1917-1964.

Samuel Jefferys, Charles W. (compiler). *A Catalogue of the Sigmund Samuel Collection of Canadiana and Americana.* Toronto: Ryerson, 1948.

Spendlove, *Face of Early Canada*

Spendlove, F. St. George. *The Face of Early Canada . . . .* Toronto: Ryerson, [1958].

Stokes Stokes, I. N. Phelps, and Daniel C. Haskell. *American Historical Prints: Early Views of American Cities, etc. From the Phelps Stokes and Other Collections.* New York: New York Public Library, 1932.